Praise for *High Performance Strategies*

CW00531455

❚❚ There are two mission-critical roles in business that often universities and most further education institutes do not cover in their faculties: the CEO and sales. Without these two vital roles performing, failure is never far away.

I have had the benefit of being 'sold' to by Russell whilst serving on the board of IPC Media. I bought and bought willingly, and he ensured his organisation at the time delivered all they said they would – and more.

Two things stood out for us. First he defined a problem we had not realised we had, by using our language and defining what success would look and feel like. Secondly and vitally, he was so easy to do business with for all levels of the organisation. A novel mixture of expertise, passion and process that remained with the business to this day.

The huge lesson learned for all of us was that when it comes to sales 'one size fits no one'. No one naturally wants to be sold to, but everyone wants to feel that they are buying the right product or service that solves their dilemma, or delivers their desired opportunity.

Russell has authored a book that is not so much to be read but experienced. You will want to share this with your sales force immediately.

Unmissable!
RENÉ CARAYOL, BUSINESS GURU

High Performance Sales Strategies

High Performance Sales Strategies

Powerful ways to win new business

Russell Ward

PEARSON

Harlow, England • London • New York • Boston • San Francisco • Toronto • Sydney
Auckland • Singapore • Hong Kong • Tokyo • Seoul • Taipei • New Delhi
Cape Town • São Paulo • Mexico City • Madrid • Amsterdam • Munich • Paris • Milan

PEARSON EDUCATION LIMITED
Edinburgh Gate
Harlow CM20 2JE
United Kingdom
Tel: +44 (0)1279 623623
Web: **www.pearson.com/uk**

First published 2014 (print and electronic)

© Russell Ward 2014 (print and electronic)

The right of Russell Ward to be identified as author of this work has been asserted by him in accordance with the Copyright, Designs and Patents Act 1988.
Pearson Education is not responsible for the content of third-party internet sites.

ISBN: 978-0-273-79285-7 (print)
      978-0-273-79471-4 (PDF)
      978-0-273-79472-1 (ePub)

British Library Cataloguing-in-Publication Data
A catalogue record for the print edition is available from the British Library

Library of Congress Cataloging-in-Publication Data
Ward, Russell, Sales consultant.
    High performance sales strategies : powerful ways to win new business / Russell Ward.
        --Edition One. pages cm
    Includes bibliographical references and index.
    ISBN 978-0-273-79285-7 (print) – ISBN (invalid) 978-0-273-79471-4 (PDF) –
ISBN (invalid) 978-0-273-79472-1 (ePub)
    1. Selling. 2. Strategic planning. 3. Sales personnel--Training of. I. Title.
    HF5438.25.W2847 2014
    658.8'02--dc23
                                    2013031117

10 9 8 7 6 5 4 3 2 1
17 16 15 14 13

Cover design by Two Associates
Print edition typeset in 11pt Myriad Pro by 3
Print edition printed and bound in Great Britain by Henry Ling Ltd., at the Dorset Press, Dorchester, Dorset

NOTE THAT ANY PAGE CROSS REFERENCES REFER TO THE PRINT EDITION

Contents

About the author

To say the author Russell Ward is passionate about ethical sales would be an understatement. He bought and sold property for nine years before moving into sales when the market crashed in 1989. His career spans from selling Christmas trees, carpet cleaning and helium balloons door-to-door to being European Sales Director at MAID plc. There he developed a sales force of 165 across 13 countries in two years from scratch which returned the fastest growth in the industry in the UK of £26m in 1996. He was a highly successful Sales Director for 11 years in four different industries before starting Silent Edge Ltd in 2002.

Having spent £700,000 on sales training courses that delivered no long term change in behaviour, and realising that the sales training industry was intent on flogging their sheep-dip courses with little concern if anyone used their learning or desire to prove return on investment, he realised that all sales directors (as he was) were focussed on lag KPI and performance against target data. There was no lead data available to them that they could use to improve their lag data. No-one was measuring sales capability.

Silent Edge is now one of the world's leading brands in sales transformation and talent management. Russell created a unique methodology that assesses sales and sales management capability across every sales role, and in every industry in the world against best practice that he defined. Tens of thousands of sales people and managers have been evaluated using Silent Edge's leading-edge bespoke technology in the last ten years. This led to ground-breaking research published in 2008 with

Cranfield School of Management entitled 'Do you know who your best sales people are?' which was later published in the *Harvard Business Review* in December 2010.

Pursuing his desire to make sales a profession that is respected and understood and to have professional qualifications in the sales industry, the methodology which is written about in this book is fast becoming the sales standard in the UK and is used by major organisations globally. Russell also wants children to aspire to sales as a career and to have sales taught in schools. To that end Russell and his company Silent Edge worked with Cranbrook School in Kent to teach 20 of their students how to sell as a result of which two of them were placed into sales roles when they left school. His belief is that if all children were taught how to sell then the GDP of the UK would be a lot higher and Blue Chip companies and SMEs would be far more successful in their quest for revenues.

Foreword

Selling and sales are increasingly recognised as vital elements in driving the growth that is desperately needed to lift most Western economies out of the current recessionary times. This recognition has led to a wave of books extolling the virtues of a certain type of sales person, a specific sales process or just emphasising the fact that everyone needs to be selling in order to be successful.

This book – and the concept of the Critical Hour – is different because it actually brings evidence-based insight to the actual moments when a sale is made. Of course, no one is questioning the benefits of having a process, a plan or a sales methodology, but these are but garnishes to the main course of getting face to face with a potential customer and having a relevant conversation that will ultimately result in you doing business together … this is selling and this is the Critical Hour.

I have had the opportunity to use the approaches described throughout this book in sales teams across different countries, sectors and types of sale. The changes in sales behaviours that I have witnessed have been astounding. The most pleasing for me was to see the reaction of 'WAIDHA' sales people – these are the sales people who have over ten years of sales experience, have probably worked at several large organisations and have been through several proprietary training courses. When you tell these sales people that there is a new initiative, their immediate reaction is 'What Am I Doing Here Again?' But by using the tools and techniques described, and by assessing their Critical Hour, they very quickly realised that this was not just another 'sheep-dip' sales training scheme.

In fact it was in this population that I saw the biggest behaviour change and the largest improvement in results. While they were already good performers and had developed a certain style, there were always areas of their performance in that Critical Hour that could be improved. Meanwhile, the less experienced sales people, who were often more open to being assessed and developed, saw this as a practical and objective approach to their personal development.

The Critical Hour is different from anything I have seen in sales before. Whether you want to improve your ability to sell yourself and your ideas at work, or if you are already a budding sales star, this is a structured approach that will help you achieve your sales potential.

NICK PORTER
GLOBAL SALES DIRECTOR
RENTOKIL INITIAL

Introduction

Sales is a strange profession that employs millions of people, and yet one which has no qualifications or standards. It is something I have studied and immersed myself in all my life since I was 19 years old.

Sales to me is one of the most challenging and yet exciting professions in the world. I love the feeling of closing a deal with a prospect that is as excited about working with us as we are with them. It is wonderful to start new relationships that flourish and develop into long-term partnerships. It makes everyone feel good and it is why I love sales.

I am so passionate about it that I created a company called Silent Edge to really help sales become a profession that people will respect and that school leavers would aspire to. I wanted to improve the way in which people sold and I wanted to be able to measure live sales and sales management capability – not just look at the numbers achieved, but be able to assess sales skills and behaviours. We use this data to provide training exactly where it is needed and managers use it to coach their staff and embed behavioural change.

The ethos of this approach is that 'you can't fix a problem if you don't know what the problem is'. Having spent 11 years as a sales director buying 'sheep-dip' training courses, I realised that training companies were all too keen to offer me training without any idea of what my problems were. They were (and most still are) only interested in flogging me courses as it suited their business model. In contrast, this book will help you to get a proven, straightforward and highly effective way of developing new business, leaving nothing to chance and ensuring you win every deal that is a genuine opportunity. What I don't discuss is things like presentation skills, i.e. how to project your voice, stand and move when presenting, etc.

Most people don't understand the complexity of sales, think all sales people are like door-to-door high-pressure wide boys, and have no idea what an amazing, interesting, lucrative and funny career it can be. And yet there are more people employed in sales than any other profession and sales is the lifeblood of every company in the world. Many people are not even aware that everyone sells on a daily basis. In 2013 there was a global survey of 10,000 people by researchers at Qualtrics who found that we spend 40 per cent of our time at work conducting non-product or service selling – persuading, influencing and convincing others (see http://metro.co.uk/2013/04/10/for-sale-one-individual-in-good-condition-how-we-sell-ourselves-every-day-3589049). What they called 'moving' others to your way of thinking. They worked out that we spend 24 minutes of every hour 'moving' others. They also found that 13 per cent of the EU's 200 million workforce earn a living through selling and 1 in 10 people in Britain work in sales – that's 3 million out of a 30 million workforce. It's 1 in 8 in Japan, with 8.6 million people in sales.

Billions are spent on training sales people every year by putting them on to courses for a few days in the belief that they will take on board all the learning and will be applying it brilliantly as business as usual from that point on. Ludicrous!

Up to mid-2008 most industries were booming and had been doing really well for ten years or more. Each time they took on a sales person they took more orders. In mid-2008 there were one million 'professional' sales people in the UK but due to the fact that companies had been so hungry for reps most were not trained properly. There was no need to spend money on sales training as there was no pain – no need when the orders were flooding in.

When the recession bit in mid-2008, however, the order taking stopped and the selling therefore had to start, as suddenly there was a competitive market demanding return on investment (ROI) and lower prices. The need to know how to sell properly could not be more pertinent, and yet of those who do sell so few know what good looks like, and hardly any have been properly trained.

This book has been written for new business sales people who operate and sell in the business-to-business (B2B) market, i.e. businesses that sell to businesses. This is because you need a more sophisticated sales process and methodology to sell to businesses as it takes longer than selling to consumers.

You could use these strategies for some business-to-consumer (B2C) sales situations, but B2C is very different and so you might not find my suggestions as effective. The reason for this is that the consumer sale is normally quite impulsive. Typical situations are sales in retail shops, restaurants, cafés, bars, car showrooms, door-to-door sales people, telesales to people in their homes – situations where the decision to buy is going to be made in seconds, minutes, hours or occasionally in days. The vast majority of people that sell in the B2C world are a transient population – students, part-time workers looking to earn a bit more for a short time, people on the first rung of the ladder of sales or business and the like. Due to their temporary nature, companies are not keen to invest heavily in sophisticated sales training courses to develop their skills, so the consumer experience is rarely a good one.

B2B sales decisions take a lot longer. A decision might be quick, a matter of days or weeks, but many take months (or even years) to be made and the sale to be completed. There is therefore a much more sophisticated process needed to do a B2B sale. Many of the interpersonal skills discussed in this book can, however, also be applied to ongoing relationships with existing clients.

Author acknowledgement

I would like to thank Lance Mortimer and Paul James for contributing to some sections of this book. Lance and Paul work at Silent Edge and are involved in, or organising the delivery of, Critical Hour training for all our clients.

Publisher's acknowledgement

We are grateful to the following for permission to reproduce copyright material:

Changingminds.org for the list of different ways to conduct a close on pages 134–5.

In some instances we have been unable to trace the owners of copyright material, and we would appreciate any information that would enable us to do so.

1

What is the Critical Hour?

Would you like to vastly improve your chances in a new business meeting, confident that you'll win that business within the hour? If you manage a sales team, how would you like to improve the ability of your whole team when it comes to winning new business? However good a sales person you are, I'm willing to bet that through this book I can give you a more effective strategy, improve your selling process and offer additional techniques and tactics that will improve your sales performance.

In my experience, very few people know how to be truly outstanding in a new business meeting, and say and do exactly the right things to optimise their chances of walking away with a deal. This book will either confirm that you're following the right methodology and will without doubt improve your skillset, or it will set you on the right path so you become successful in every new business encounter. It will give you a huge competitive advantage.

Sales is a much misunderstood role. It's not a singular skill. You need to be good at a multitude of different aspects to be an accomplished sales person. The core DNA of a sales person is tenacity, resilience and curiosity. If you have those attributes, the next step to high performance selling is the process and the skillset that need to be learned by heart.

Some sales people are born to sell. They seem to have an innate ability. Most sales people, however, are made – the ability is developed through learning the correct processes of good selling. A sound, professional process is vital, even if you are born with enthusiasm and the ability to persuade. Without it you'll be nothing more than a nuisance product pusher – especially in a new business situation.

A new business person is often compared to, or called, a hunter. If you think back to the cave-dwelling days when the man would go out and hunt for the family dinner, when they brought back 'the kill' they would pass it to their partner or family for them to prepare and cook it. They were only interested in 'the kill' and once achieved would have no further interest in it other than eating it.

The other role often referred to in sales is a farmer or account manager. They do not like going out for 'the kill' but would much rather nurture a client and help solve problems and issues.

I am a new business person or hunter – I really enjoy closing the deal. I have thought long and hard about the process of new business selling and that's what *High Performance Sales Strategies* is all about. I will break down exactly what you have to do to be brilliant in your live meetings, which I call the **Critical Hour,** and I will describe how I came to develop the concept in Chapter 2.

Let's look at a Critical Hour

A new business meeting usually lasts no more than an hour. Have you ever thought about what you need to pack into that hour to make it so compelling that the prospect wants to buy from you every time? You probably realise how important that initial hour is, but I strongly believe it's absolutely essential to get it right.

How you sell and deliver a compelling value proposition in those 60 minutes in front of your prospect will determine whether you do business together.

And yet so many people get it wrong, take it for granted or simply do not know what to do for the best.

In order to define all the best practice elements that go into the Critical Hour I conducted many months of research before creating a model of it (see Figure 1.1). We will return to this model later in the chapter.

In the 2012 London Olympics the British cycling team had their best ever result. The head coach was Dave Brailsford and when he was interviewed after the event he was asked how they did it. He explained that it was all about **marginal gains**. If you can do everything 1 per cent better, then when you put all those 1 per cents together, it makes a huge gain.

Many things the team did were obvious, but they went further, like taking their own pillows with them as they travelled the country, staying in hotels when going to different events, to ensure they had a good sleep, or cleaning the area between thumb and first finger properly to ensure maximum hygiene.

This breakdown into minute detail of exactly what you need to do to be brilliant at selling, and doing all the small things as well as the big things to the best possible standard, was what I worked on back in 2003.

In my 30 years in sales I have sold at all levels and managed large sales teams (the biggest team being 165 people across 13 European countries, which I recruited and trained myself in two years). As a sales consultant and strategist, I have worked with many blue-chip organisations as clients and have come across thousands of sales people with large pipelines (i.e. projects at various stages of development).

All these sales people face a familiar problem: lots of prospects, great positive pipelines, but not enough of the deals are closing.

Figure 1.1 Critical Hour model

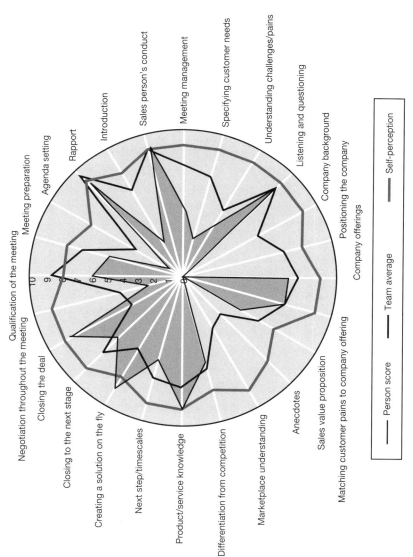

Labels around the model (clockwise):
Qualification of the meeting
Meeting preparation
Agenda setting
Rapport
Introduction
Sales person's conduct
Meeting management
Specifying customer needs
Understanding challenges/pains
Listening and questioning
Company background
Positioning the company
Company offerings
Matching customer pains to company offering
Sales value proposition
Anecdotes
Marketplace understanding
Differentiation from competition
Product/service knowledge
Next step/timescales
Creating a solution on the fly
Closing to the next stage
Closing the deal
Negotiation throughout the meeting

Legend:
Person score — Team average — Self-perception

Figure 1.2 Connecting pipeline to skills and behaviours

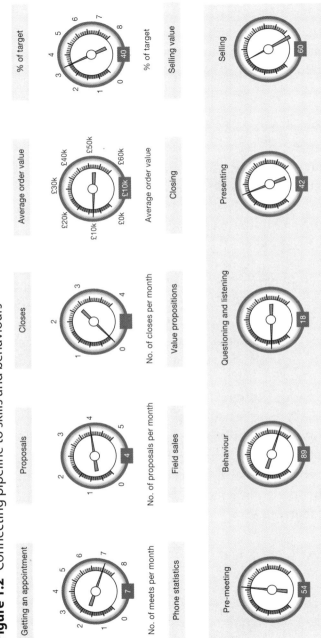

Figure 1.2 shows a classic case with sales teams. The top line shows that the sales person is going out on a good number of meetings each month, which are converting into proposals. However the proposals are not turning into closes, and the average order value per sale is poor, indicating the sales person is selling on price and not hitting target.

The second row of Figure 1.2 shows why this is happening: they do not prepare for the meeting properly, and although their selling behaviour is good (common with most sales people) they are not listening to the client or asking questions. Therefore they do not have a platform from which to present and build a value proposition, even though they are trying hard to close.

The problem is that the sales person is simply a product pusher. Because they are not questioning the client, they are not finding out the client's needs and pains. So the client will simply say 'Send me a proposal', but will have no intention of ever responding after the meeting. The sales person then returns to the office and enters the value of that proposal into their pipeline, which never closes.

Sound familiar? If so, then you or your team are getting your Critical Hour wrong. Your prospects are politely asking for a proposal but then never return your calls or emails once you've sent it. That's because they do not feel compelled to buy from you so have either done nothing about the sale, or will have bought from your competitors.

If you get your Critical Hour wrong, you face competition from a number of angles:

● **The client does nothing**. The prospect decides to do nothing and so does not take your product or service, or anyone else's for that matter – they just carry on as they were.

- **They do it internally**. The prospect decides they have the resources internally to create something similar to what your product or service can offer. So they don't buy from you.
- **They buy from your competitors**. The prospect chooses to go with a product or service from one of your competitors and you lose the deal.

It is important that you see all three options as equal; understanding how to sell in your Critical Hour will enable you to create a sense of urgency and need that will clearly differentiate you and your company against all three choices above.

This book is based on a methodology I created and will break down the Critical Hour into component parts. There are many different things you need to be doing in a new business meeting within that hour, and knowing what these are and how to do them will ensure success and revenue growth.

I've seen fantastic results from my Critical Hour methodology, including the following:

- A team in Cable and Wireless grew from £750,000 per month order intake to £4m per month in just six months – that's 450 per cent growth.
- Barclays Business grew 39 per cent in 12 months and had a per cent increase in customer satisfaction.
- Reed Specialist Recruitment achieved a 900 per cent return on their investment over a 12-month period.
- After three years of flat growth a company called Sematron grew from £12m to £18m in a year and then a further 35 per cent the next year.

Not only does the methodology work commercially, but it also draws on research by Cranfield School of Management (2008) and Ashridge Business School (2007) with results published in *Harvard Business Review*, December 2010. For the research at Cranfield, we analysed 800 blue-chip sales people at work using the best practice observations defined in the Critical Hour. It identified the following eight different behavioural traits in sales people globally (you can download a copy from **www.silentedge.co.uk**).

SOCIALISER

Socialiser

These people chat, drink tea and coffee and eat a lot of biscuits. They display hardly any sales skills other than rapport. An example of this type of sales person is one that pops in to see their client each week or month, has a long chat about holidays, golf, the weather or other such small talk, asks if the client would like any more of the product or service, and when they get a no just say, 'Bye – see you next month' and move on.

AGGRESSOR

Aggressor

These people are bullies. They are high-pressure, aggressive sales people who are only interested in their commission, are not concerned about what the customer needs and will sell them anything they can whether they need it or not just to make the sale. These clients may be put off from purchasing because of the 'hard sell',. The research certainly shows that pressure selling is not a great way to achieve sales as these were the second least successful behaviours studied. Examples include the persistent shop assistant ('Can I help you? That one is really nice') where the customer simply walks away from the sale unless they are very strongly motivated to buy.

NARRATOR

These sales people have learnt the script and stick to it. However, if you ask them a question that is off the script, they will not be able to answer and will be found wanting. They will look unknowledgeable and unhelpful when faced with a bit of probing from their potential customer. That will result in the customer losing interest and confidence in the sales person and therefore the company they represent. Lost sale.

Narrator

PRODUCT PUSHER

These people are totally focused on features and benefits of the products or service they are promoting. They know everything about *their* offering but do nothing

Product Pusher

to ask any questions of the customer or find out about what they need or what their pains are. The customer will probably ask for a proposal to be polite, but they will have no intention of even reading it, let alone answering the countless follow-up calls they will get from the sales person.

STORYTELLER

This sales person is quite good at selling but talks too much. They give far too many stories (case studies or anecdotes) about how good their products or services are. Using cases and anecdotes is essential but an overload becomes too much for the potential customer and they switch off. These sales people also tend to miss what

Storyteller

their customer is asking for, their body language, and buying or boredom signals as they are so focused on the success of their company etc.

CONSULTANT

The behaviours that these people display are particularly valuable where the situation calls for complex or solution selling where the offering may be complicated and multi-dimensional. The sales person may be selling to multiple decision makers or influencers

Consultant

and the time it takes to agree a deal may be considerable (often these deals will take nine months or more). People with these behaviours are particularly good at overcoming objections, which may also make them good at cross-selling within existing accounts.

PRODUCT CLOSER

This is someone who can really sell products or services. They listen and can think on their feet quickly, providing customers with excellent value propositions that suit their business needs. If you need someone to just sell high volumes and uncomplicated products, or lots of repeat sales to existing customers, then

Product Closer

this is the type of sales person you're looking for. Their weakness is that they tend to rely too much on 'winging it' in the sales meeting.

EXPERT

These people are adept at long-term, multi-decision maker, complex solution selling but could probably also do transactional sales if need be. They exhibit exemplary listening, negotiation and sales value proposition skills and their ability to think on

Expert

their feet and offer complex solutions in a simple and compelling manner is second to none. If you have people with expert behaviours, think about how they could mentor and coach your less capable sales people and pass on their expertise.

Figure 1.3 shows research on how three different types of sales areas (new business, telesales and account management) are made up of the different traits. What is shocking to see here is that 57 per cent of new business people, 70 per cent of telesales people and 50 per cent of account managers sat in the lowest four categories of socialiser, aggressor, narrator and product pusher. These were blue-chip sales people on high basic salaries plus commission. Alarmingly, the organisations studied were largely unaware of the poor calibre of their sales teams.

Figure 1.3 Sales area traits

	Storyteller	Aggressor	Narrator	Product pusher		Storyteller	Consultant	Product closer	Expert
New business	13%	5%	16%	23%		6%	15%	10%	12%
Telesales	26%	6%	16%	22%		11%	11%	6%	2%
Account mgt	22%	8%	12%	8%		8%	16%	24%	4%

Source: Cranfield School of Management

The findings of the Cranfield research demonstrated how poor the seemingly best sales people in the UK were in their Critical Hour, and how companies really don't have any visibility of what they are saying or doing in their live meetings.

If you're a manager of sales people or perhaps a business owner or director of a small to medium-sized enterprise (SME), then ask yourself when you last saw a member of your team sell throughout the full extent of their Critical Hour. If you have been out with them, were you able to not interrupt or take over the meeting? Did you see them sell all the way through to the end?

If you don't observe someone carry and sell throughout their Critical Hour without interruption, then how can you possibly coach or develop them? Interestingly, 95 per cent of accompanied field visits by a manager with a member of their sales team are taken over by the manager.

TNT were part of the research study we did with Cranfield and the manager of their corporate team, Bill Thompson, wrote the Foreword to the study report. In my initial Critical Hour with Bill he was so impressed with my approach of objective assessment of sales capability that he asked for a change development programme. However, it took him over a year to give me the order because he felt that he knew his corporate team of sales people intimately, as he had worked with most of them for many years, and so doubted what benefit he would gain from the assessment. This is what he said in the Foreword:

> *'I thought I knew the capability of my team, what they were good at and not so good at. The assessment confirmed some of my thinking, gave me fresh information and proved some of my thinking to be incorrect. In this respect the assessment exceeded all my expectations.'*

Most companies have no idea how their sales people are performing in their Critical Hours. If you think about how many Critical Hours are conducted every day in business and how many will be terrible (as per the statistics above), you can see why this high-performance sales approach will be so beneficial to you.

The eureka moment for the Critical Hour

When I started Silent Edge in 2002 I offered my time as an interim or consultant sales director. Not the best business model, as I couldn't work with more than two clients at one time, and prospecting for new clients was tough because I was shadowing clients all the time.

One of my clients was a communications company based in Skipton. They had made no new business sales in 18 months, and all the revenues were client driven, so they asked me to come and work out why.

There was a sales team of six people and a sales director. The sales director had been managing the clients by himself and had not spent much time managing the sales team. He was younger than them and the sales guys thought they knew better.

I went out with them all on two new business meetings each and was horrified by what I saw. I also met the clients, and after some analysis of all the meetings, proposals and performance against target statistics, as well as the value propositions and collateral, I wrote a report for the CEO.

As you might expect, he was rather alarmed about the report so he asked to meet me for dinner to discuss my recommendation that I sack his whole sales force other than the sales director, redo all his propositions and start afresh.

He asked me 'How do you know you're right in your conclusion? Because if you're wrong and I go with your report, then I could get sacked!' Despite the confidence I had in my own report, my sales experience and what I had seen with my own eyes, he kept asking why he should believe me.

'Let me tell you about the process I used to come to this conclusion' I said. I proceeded to describe how I had been out on two meetings with each of the sales people and they were dreadful – all gift of the gab, chatty but there was no questioning and listening – the meetings were all about them and their product. Terrible! Worse still, many meetings were not even qualified properly, with the person they were speaking to not having any decision-making capability at all.

My experience had taught me that there is a particular process and path to follow in each new business meeting, and if you follow that then you are a successful sales person.

'How long were the meetings?' asked the CEO

'An hour each' I said

'That was a pretty critical hour for them then' said the CEO

That was it! The Critical Hour!

The other nightmare was that each company believed by taking me on, their sales would automatically go through the roof in a very short space of time. There was normally so much wrong with their sales methods that I realised it would be a better use of my efforts to develop a more meaningful framework for sales people to become more effective.

Having perfected a name for the Critical Hour, I began to work out in great detail all the things you need to be good at to be brilliant in your Critical Hour, which is the basis of my methodology (these dimensions are discussed in detail in Chapter 4). The first thing I did was to create a method to measure performance and came up with the scorecard. The first scorecard I created was for new business and this approach is now used, along with the technology platform, to measure how good people are at selling.

In Figure 1.4 you can see that the sales person has been compared to best practice (a maximum score of 10 in each dimension) and what they think of their own ability in the Critical Hour. They will have gone online and completed a self-assessment. They can also see how they compare with the average score of others in a similar role in their company. It is easy for the manager to give feedback on their capability compared to best practice, the team (as indicated by the team average) and the sales person's self-perception (which is often inflated).

Most sales people have no idea about their capability benchmarked against best practice, so this is a powerful method to identify their strengths and weaknesses and create an individual personal development plan for them.

In this book I only cover new business sales, but I have also created many other scorecards covering every sales role in the world today. These are tailored by industry and also by country culture, for example:

- All telephone sales roles – inbound, outbound, telemarketing, sales through service, customer service in call centres or small teams.
- Account management – transactional sales (sales cycle up to six months), complex sales (sales cycle up to 18 months and high-value deals with multi-decision makers) and super complex (£50m+).
- Technical pre-sales.

Figure 1.4 Sales person's concept of own ability in the Critical Hour

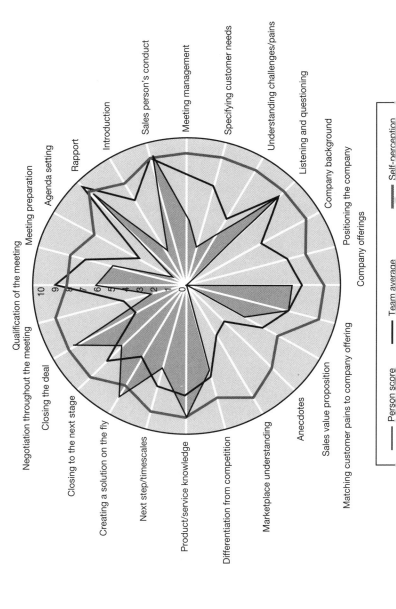

- Alliance, partner, channel or third-party sales (i.e. you sell to someone who will then sell your product and service direct to the buyer).
- Sales management – either management of frontline sales staff or managers of managers. This differs between call centres and field sales teams.
- Sales leadership.

In all, Silent Edge has over 450 different scorecards that have been created over eight years. By the end of 2012 tens of thousands of people globally had been assessed using them. The minimum impact they have made since we started to license our approach for managers to use with their staff is 8.6 per cent growth in revenues in a year. That's the minimum. The biggest so far was a mobile telecoms company, whose call centre of 250 people increased their net profit by £20m or 20 per cent in a year – we turned their call centre operation from a service centre into a sales force.

Your return on investment (ROI)

I refer to return on investment (ROI) a lot. I believe that most people understand what this is and why it is so important, but I just want to labour the point for a short time.

The world is constantly changing. It took 50 years for the industrial revolution to make an impact and 25 years for the communications revolution to make its impact. Technology is moving at such a pace and everything is getting faster. For example, it took Google to grow to the size of Microsoft in half the time and Microsoft didn't see them coming. Then Facebook did the same thing and grew to Google's size in half the time and Google didn't see them coming. Then there was Twitter, and so the list will continue.

The interesting thing is that many of these new companies were started in someone's bedroom. That was inconceivable 20 years ago. Social media is now mainstream and is changing the way we communicate, and adversely affecting the ability of many young people to converse with those they don't know.

The point is that the world has changed and will continue to do so. In days gone by it would have been fine to demonstrate your product to a customer and they would buy it. Through the advent of the internet it is possible for any customer to look at your competitors; 20 years ago that wasn't possible, so a customer might never know that they could have bought the product or service a lot cheaper elsewhere. Competition is now fierce and very price sensitive.

To close business, you now need to be able to demonstrate real ROI and, unless you can do that for a prospect or customer, then you have no hope.

I will emphasise understanding the customer's pains a lot later on, but here are some now for consideration:

- Can you save the customer time?
- Can you save the customer money?
- Can you create efficiencies that will affect both of the above?
- Can you increase their profitability or margin?
- Can you increase their revenues?
- Can you enhance their brand value?

If you can't do any of the above then it is unlikely the customer will buy from you. If you can do the above but don't articulate it clearly to them, then you will also lose that deal.

In the depths of the current recession we are experiencing the common buying behaviours that we normally see in these times:

- Most decisions require a business case.
- More people are involved in making the decision (many you will never meet).
- Procurement (a department that hardly existed in most companies 20 years ago) will make competitive comparisons on price.
- Decisions take a long time and often stall unless a sense of urgency and value can be created.

So demonstrating ROI and the ability to describe it in a compelling manner that really demonstrates value has never been more important than now. A clear description of how to do that follows, so that you win in your Critical Hour and close more and more new business deals.

Why it is important to be objective

Subjectivity

How often do you meet someone who will give you their opinion of a person, only for you to find out a while later that they were completely wrong? Subjective views can be dangerous and yet we frequently rely on them without challenge.

If three people were to watch a car go past a window and were asked to describe what they had seen, they will likely give three completely different descriptions.

People see things differently. You see things through your own paradigm. Things that have happened to you shape the way you see things.

I remember a story that Brian Mayne (the innovator of the Goal Mapping methodology, who runs a company called Lift International) tells about going to the local pub to see some friends, one of whom had a teenage girl with her. They were all enjoying themselves, having a laugh, when an old man came into the pub and sat down in a chair near the group. Brian noticed that he was staring at the teenage girl, so he caught the eye of the old man and 'stared him out'. The old man looked away quickly. This repeated itself a number of times and after a while Brian found he was getting really uptight. 'Who is this pervert staring at my friend?' he thought, and started to think about confronting him. The girl spotted Brian staring at the old man and leaned over and said, 'That's my uncle; he's here to pick me up and is early'.

Subjective views form the basis of many opinions that people carry around within themselves all the time, transfer on to others and potentially misuse.

Have you ever jumped to a conclusion about something or someone only to be completely wrong? The number of times that someone's view can become fact is scary. Each of us has our own world view about what is right and what is wrong, what happened and what did not. Indeed the memory is a very fallible tool, open to decay, distortion and suggestion. Over even the briefest of moments, with the simplest of distractions, we can easily muddle reality with our internal view of the world to come up with a conclusion about how things are. An example of this is the variability of eye-witness testimony.

In my company we have a mantra:

'Seek first to understand before jumping to conclusions.'

If you adopt this mantra it can be life-changing, as you will discover very different reasons for someone's behaviour or reaction.

For senior managers this mantra is essential as they're often removed from the frontline and are dependent on what people tell them. Add to that people telling you what you want, or what they want you to hear, and you have a dangerous concoction.

So it is always good to check things out and make a practice of seeking to understand to get the real and clear picture before jumping to conclusions or assuming anything.

Assumption

An old chairman of mine once told me, 'Assumption is the mother of all fuck-ups.' That couldn't be more true, and assumption seems to be something that sales people are blessed with!

Assumption is caused by not enough detail or understanding of the actual facts. Combine that with the reality that one of the weakest areas for sales people is their questioning and listening skills, and you can understand why pipelines are not accurately forecast and deals do not close.

From the research we did with Cranfield in 2008, the most common type of sales person came out as the product pusher person – someone who is a walking, talking brochure. They can talk about the product and industry till the cows come home, but don't do any selling that connects their offering to the client's needs and pains. They assume the client will want to hear about what they have to offer. Madness!

So often in sales pitches the sale person has not done enough fact-finding and therefore does not have the platform on which to build a compelling value proposition that will entice the customer to buy. They base their proposals on what they think they have heard or what they have interpreted from what the client said, if indeed the sales person even makes an attempt to put a value proposition in place at all. They make assumptions because they are too timid, lazy or simply lack the know-how to ask challenging and searching questions to get the full picture. Inadequate preparation and skill deficiency are the real enemies here that need to be attacked.

Why objectivity is important

When I started Silent Edge in 2002 I typed 'sales competency' into Google and three hits came back that were relevant. As of July 2013 there are 8,610,000 hits – many of which are still not relevant.

Companies are now, more than ever before, wanting to measure and ascertain the capability of their sales teams. The astonishing thing is that all of them are using a subjective method of assessment that involves self-assessment, plus the 'more sophisticated', assessment by your manager, with a gap comparison of the two (180-degree analysis). Eventually these companies will find out that they are wasting their time.

When I developed the first scorecard for the Critical Hour in 2004 I defined 16 elements that sat within it (see Figure 2.1) and I would score how good I thought someone was on a 1 to 5 point scale – 5 being very good. I worked out that assessing someone in two sales meetings would give a good average footprint of their capability. More than two meetings and the footprint didn't change.

Figure 2.1 Critical Hour scorecard: early version

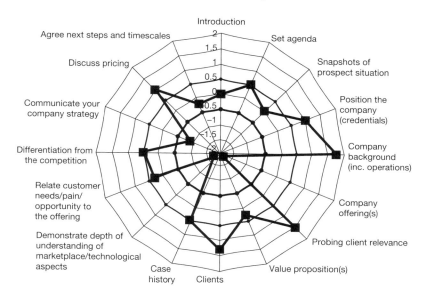

One day, however, I could not do both meetings with a senior business development guy so a colleague did one meeting and I did the other. When we came to write the report about the sales guy, she had scored him very high and I had scored him very low. The results were polarised. When we discussed it, it turned out that his pitch was the same but it was his treatment of us that differed. He had taken my colleague out for lunch and was charming and delightful to her, so she thought he was lovely. With me, however, he was rude, shut the meeting room door in my face and didn't introduce me. I didn't like him from the minute I met him and this was reflected in my score.

At that point I realised that the model I had created was not commercial. It was flawed by one of the common psychological issues in the workplace, that of the 'horns and halos' effect, otherwise known as subjective bias. This phenomenon happens all the time and the frightening thing about it is that we often do not even know we are biased.

First, let's consider the reasons why subjectivity produces data that is incorrect:

- When a manager does an assessment they are being asked to give their view of an individual's capability. If that manager does not like one of their team then they are likely to score harshly. If they get on with them well, they will be generous.
- One manager may have very high standards whereas another may not. So the standard of marking will differ.
- Often there may be 60 or more competencies that managers need to score, which can take a long time. If assessing a lot of employees it's natural for people to lose interest and concentration, so the quality of the

assessments will deteriorate considerably as the day goes on.

● People see and interpret things in different ways.

The end result will be an incorrect set of data after a pointless box-ticking exercise. This is borne out in research published in May 2012 by Silent Edge **www.silentedge.co.uk**. This showed that:

● **71 per cent** of organisations that took part in the research are using a competency framework within their organisation.

● **33 per cent** of organisations measure the right competencies.

● **35 per cent** of HR directors are unable to identify any outcomes from using a competency framework.

● **8 per cent** of the competency frameworks in use today involve objective measures and result in positive behavioural change.

As seen in Figure 2.2, approximately 50 per cent of companies see very little or no benefit in terms of improved behaviour or impact as a result of using a subjective competency framework.

Figure 2.2 Change in behaviour using competency framework

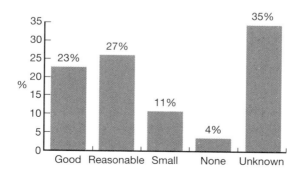

It is clear that the need for an objective way of assessing someone is of paramount importance. This is the basis of the best practice new business approach and the basis of the Critical Hour model.

Creating an objective competency framework

I had to create an objective way of scoring capability to develop a framework that could be used consistently and sold commercially.

In order to create an objective way of scoring behaviour I had to start by defining what 'good' looks like in detail. So I took the 16 elements I was using in my subjective framework and broke them down into a lot more detail.

The first framework I wrote was for a new business meeting (where the Critical Hour was born). I realised that there were more than 16 elements: they grew to 29 and I called them dimensions. Then I worked out all the different skills and behaviours that need to be carried out for a sales person to be excellent in those 29 dimensions – which turned out to number 170 in total.

The next step was to define the overall competencies in which the 29 dimensions would reside, and so I created five of them – pre-meeting, behaviour, questioning and listening, presenting and selling.

So now I had a framework that I could use to compare the performance of any sales person in their Critical Hour. In order to make it a commercial proposition I then had to create a technology platform that could be used to capture the data and then automatically display the results online. That took two years to develop in its most basic form and has taken a further seven years to evolve into the sophisticated coaching platform that it is today.

The technology is now used by sales managers to assess their staff in live meetings and role plays. If the sales person performs one of the observations in a meeting they get a tick against that observation, and if they don't do what is defined in the framework then they get a cross. The system is completely binary – they either did or they didn't do it. So it is objective.

That then gives a highly detailed view of where that person's strengths and weaknesses are, which is used for training and, most importantly, coaching purposes by the manager.

And so the first ever truly objective competency framework was proudly born in 2004!

I then realised I needed to create a scorecard to assess the knowledge of the new business person relevant to their role. This identifies whether they know what they should be doing and how to behave outside the live meeting scenario – for example, how they manage and forecast a pipeline, how they report to their manager, their use of CRM systems, proposal writing, etc.

Moving on from that I created a scorecard for telephone sales. So much of a new business person's role is spent on the phone either making an appointment or looking to progress and close a deal after a meeting. So I used a similar objective approach and defined best practice for this role.

That progressed to call centre sales roles (inbound and outbound) and then customer service.

Alongside those I created account management scorecards – complex, large-value, long-term sales scorecards (deals of £1m+ and another for deals over £50m – super complex).

Then came the sales manager scorecards – manager of frontline field sales people, manager of telephone sales people, manager of managers and then sales leader (sales director).

Leonardo da Vinci once said that simplicity is the greatest sophistication. This belief was also coined and picked up by Steve Jobs as he sought to develop Apple into the incredible digital hub company it is today. The simplicity of the Critical Hour, comprising only five competencies, makes it a sophisticated tool. At Silent Edge we have found that there is no need to add unnecessary measurement criteria, because you have all the data you need.

The competencies of the Critical Hour

The Critical Hour is the product of years of development and refinement. It has taken shape over this time to become the well-oiled machine it is today. This position is the result of evaluating tens of thousands of sales people and also the academically rigorous testing of the solution by one of the UK's leading business schools.

We now know that measuring the five Critical Hour competencies will give you all the objective information you need about your sales force to fully pinpoint the areas that truly need attention and development. For example, a sales person who is consistently facing a heap of objections in the closing phase of the sale may find themselves being put on an objection-handling course. After all, that is clearly what they need, right?

Wrong. Did you ever think that the objections might arise because of the fact they have not questioned the client properly to understand what their needs and pains are, and so have not created any interest from the prospect? Or the product and its pricing is so poor that it is raising many questions? The red flag here is that the presenting problem is not always the underlying issue, yet it's the presenting that is often dealt with.

Let's go back to our sales friend above who is getting loads of objections. Is this perhaps because they have not listened well enough to understand the customer's needs? By using the Critical Hour model, we can see which competencies need attention.

The five competencies of the Critical Hour are shown in Figure 3.1.

1 **Pre-meeting**. This is all about ensuring that the meeting is worth having and it meets the required qualification criteria for having it. If so, then how you prepare with research and agreeing an agenda with the prospect

Figure 3.1 The five competencies of the Critical Hour

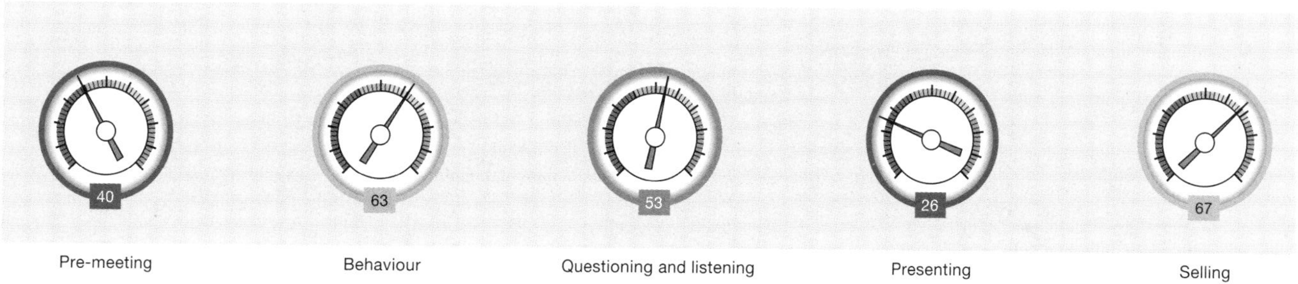

Pre-meeting	Behaviour	Questioning and listening	Presenting	Selling
40	63	53	26	67

beforehand is crucial. Finally, on the day, it is important that you look the part and present yourself well, as first impressions are key.

2 **Behaviour**. This is where we look at the sales person's conduct and behaviour throughout the meeting and how they actually manage it in terms of time and conciseness. A key part of this is rapport, at which most sales people seem to excel, and how they introduce themselves and others in their Critical Hour.

3 **Questioning and listening**. Simply allowing a client to talk about themselves and their company for ages is not listening. This competence is all about asking the right questions in the right way to uncover not only what the client thinks they need in relation to your offering, but also what their challenges and pains are. This might well result in them needing something completely different to what they expected – which you can provide – and moves you into a position of trust and strength in your Critical Hour.

4 **Presenting**. This covers not only how you present your marketplace, company and its products and services, but also how you use the earlier sections of your Critical Hour (above) to orientate your solution in a compelling way that demonstrates value to the client's business in a number of different ways. It is also how you provide evidence of how you have done this with other clients that have had similar pains and needs, and shown clear ROI as a result.

5 **Selling**. The core skills of moving a deal to a close are contained in this section. You must be able to demonstrate clarity of product and service knowledge, differentiation from the competition (internal and external), objection handling, negotiation, closing to next

steps or closing the deal itself and, most importantly, the ability to think on your feet. And you must combine all the knowledge you have garnered from the above process to convince the customer you have the right solution for them.

Figure 3.1 shows the model working in action for our sales friend. Each dial shows the sales person's performance in each of the five competencies. The figures under each dial are a percentage measured against best practice, as defined in the Critical Hour.

4

The dimensions of the Critical Hour

The purpose of the following sections is not to give you an exhaustive discourse on each dimension of the Critical Hour, but to guide you through what has been proven to be a very successful and straightforward approach to new business sales. It's a quick and simple read and if you follow this approach you will, without doubt, increase your productivity and success. Simplicity in action!

This chapter will teach you the flow, format, process and skills you need to be brilliant in new business sales. The dimensions in Figure 4.1 are what you need to cover in every new business meeting you conduct with a prospect. These 29 dimensions (which fit into the five competencies) are described in detail in this chapter. (The points marked with an asterisk in the list below do not appear on the diagram but are integral to the process.)

1 Qualification of the meeting
2 Meeting preparation
3 Personal presentation*
4 Agenda setting
5 Rapport
6 Introductions
7 Sales person's conduct
8 Meeting management
9 Specifying customer needs
10 Understanding challenges/pains
11 Listening and questioning
12 Company background
13 Positioning the company
14 Company offerings
15 Matching customer pains to company offering

Figure 4.1 Critical Hour model

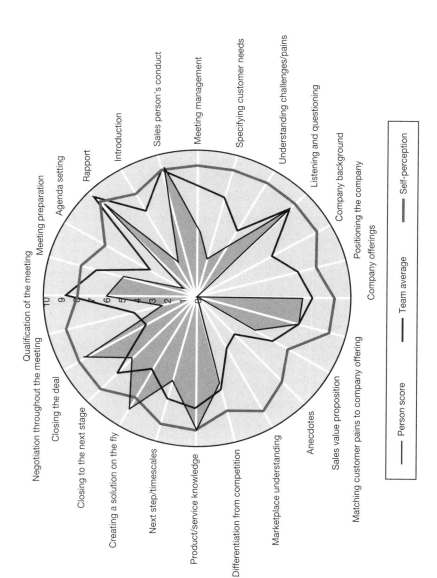

16 Case studies*

17 Sales value proposition

18 Anecdotes

19 Discussing value*

20 Marketplace understanding

21 Differentiation from competition

22 Differentiation from competition when challenged*

23 Product/service knowledge

24 Next steps/timescales

25 Objection handling*

26 Creating a solution on the fly

27 Closing to the next stage

28 Closing the deal

29 Negotiation throughout the meeting

By following this methodology you will increase the number of successful meetings you have, as well as your closing ratio and revenue growth. You will also be more time-efficient as you'll only attend meetings that are worthwhile and follow up on opportunities that you know you have a chance of closing.

1 Qualification of the meeting

Would you go out to a meeting if you didn't know who your prospect was, what they needed, whether they had the money or the time? All too often the answer to this question is yes, and the Critical Hour can go wrong just through a simple lack of qualification that it was worth going to in the first place.

Pitfalls

- **Seeing the wrong person**. The number of meetings I have seen where the wrong person is being presented to is astonishing. At the end of the meeting, when the prospect finally understands what is being sold to them, they say: 'You need to meet with Bob in finance – I think he will have a need for this as it's not really relevant to me'. It is important to make sure there is a decision maker or major influencer in the room so you can progress the deal or close it if appropriate. If you have not qualified whether the person you're seeing can make a decision, then you could have wasted a lot of unnecessary time, as you'll need to come back and meet the decision maker at a later date.

- **Finding out there's no budget**. It's also frequently the case that at the end of a presentation the client reveals they don't have any budget allocated or the funds haven't been estimated. If they have no budget then you might be better rearranging the meeting for a time when the budget is available so you can go to see someone else who has a budget and more immediate needs.

- **Organising the meeting just to look busy**. I have also seen some real horror stories where companies create a key performance indicator (KPI) based on the number of meetings someone will need to do per week. That's it – just that number. Madness! It should be number of *qualified* meetings per week, and the qualification criteria should be clearly laid out or you will have a lot of busy fools.

In all of the above instances, you risk losing time, which could delay your sales cycle (the time it takes from initiating contact with a prospect company to closing a piece of business) or, worse still, another company will seal the deal.

Step back for a moment and think about what that meeting cost. How long did it take to get? Sometimes people can spend weeks or months getting a decent appointment. Getting an appointment with anyone just for the sake of going to see a prospect is a complete waste of time and money.

If someone is paid £35,000, then being out for the day is £160, cost of travel etc. £50, time to get to the meeting £80 and daily contribution to overheads £80 – so being out for a day will have cost the company at least £370. One wasted meeting a week for 46 weeks of the year is £17,000 or 50 per cent of their base salary.

Getting the right people you need to progress your deal or make a decision should be achieved at the outset when setting up the meeting. It's not always possible, but at least make sure you've tried.

Knowing how to be more effective in meetings and then making it happen will make you more efficient and successful. It is easy from the above figure to see how the ROI by knowing the key development areas can stack up. How much would you pay right now to be able to save just a fraction of the wasted money in your sales force?

High performance tips
● **Phone first**. The more you can do over the phone prior to the meeting – to sell in, test the prospect's reaction

---

and qualify – then the better your Critical Hour will be and the more they will be looking forward to seeing you.

- **Be irresistible** – Another sure sign of unqualified meetings is cancellations and meetings moving. In these cases you have not created a compelling reason to meet so the meeting is easy to bump or cancel from the prospect's point of view.

- **Find out who your competition is**. Make sure you know if there is an incumbent competitor your prospect is working with, and if so are they happy with them? If they are seeing other companies like you, then try and find out their names. This will help you to prepare.

2 Meeting preparation

This tends to be the new business person's weakness – so few really prepare for meetings.

If two people came up to you in a bar and one didn't know you other than your name, and the other knew all about you, your family, career, hobbies etc., showed a real interest in what you do and had obviously done their research to engage you in conversation, which one are you likely get along with and warm to?

High performance tips

- Agree the objectives for the meeting with the prospect over the phone prior to the meeting.

- Get a broad understanding of their needs and budget if possible.

- Find out when their financial year starts.
- Understand the industry that your prospect works in, including latest news.
- Understand their competitors.
- Understand what competition you might be up against (including internal to the prospect, e.g. are they trying to do something themselves using their people?).
- Find out if there any past history between your company and the prospect.
- Tailor your presentation to the prospect with this information.
- Go on LinkedIn and check out the profile of the people you are seeing so you can see what their interests are and how their skills are orientated.

Doing the right preparation is not only good practice and will make you look professional and keen for their business, but it can give you an advantage since you can pretty much guarantee that your competitors are unlikely to do their research. You may also find out information that the prospect was not even aware of if you dig deep enough.

All of the above points will give you a platform not only to build rapport, but also to get a real insight into the prospect as a business, which you can leverage later on in your presentation.

3 Personal presentation

I have been in a presentation where the sales person stank so much of body odour that the prospect was visibly flinching at times. How likely do you think that sales person was to closing that piece of business?

They say that people make their mind up about a person in the first ten seconds of meeting them – taking in information about the way they look, smell, body language, expressions, the way they dress, etc.

The rule of business is to dress for success, smell nice and have a smile on your face. Sometimes that may require being smart, other times it may be appropriate to dress down for some prospects like a media company.

You're unlikely to be put off by a smart person – you quite likely to be put off by someone who looks and smells rough. Overdoing the fragrance can be equally as repellent as bad body odour. I remember in my very early days as a young sales guy, my sales manager said to me, as I stood there before him proudly sporting my half bottle of Paco Rabanne, 'Young man, remember: big smell, no sell'. I toned it down after that!

High performance tip

Take the time to make sure you look and smell nice and are well turned out.

---

4 Agenda setting

Again this is a common area of weakness in new business people.

There is a famous phrase that says, 'If you don't know where you're going then how will you get there? You wouldn't get in a car and just drive to a new destination without looking at a map and planning your journey.' This is predominantly used in goal setting but is also true of a meeting. Setting an agenda is a great way of creating clarity on what both you and the prospect would like to achieve in the meeting. Many times I have seen meetings get halfway through or further and the prospect says, 'What is the point or where are we trying to get to from this meeting?'

The objective of this meeting is to review the current status of the ABC Sales Academy programme, to discuss any critical areas and/or areas of concern and to agree next stages as required

Agenda for the Steering Group status meeting
- Review of status meeting on 4 June (minutes) – SE
- Status report on all channels (Steering Group Red, Amber, Green) – SE
- ABC missing deadlines and the impact on Silent Edge –SE
- Review of Accreditation and Evaluation programmes – ABC/SE
- Workbooks and training material – SE
- Out of scope report, including update on invoicing – SE
- Training & Development update – ABC
- AOB
- Next steps/action

Attendees:

Jo Bloggs, Jack Bloggs, Russell Ward, Mr Very Important Director, Mrs Major Decision Maker

Date: 16 July 2013

Time: 10.00–12.30pm

Location (of meeting): Large Palace, Buckingham Palace Road, London WC2

SE contact

Jo Bloggs

mobile: +44 (0) 7777 555555

email: jo.bloggs@silentedge.co.uk

ABC contact

Jack Bloggs

mobile: +44 (0) 5555 66666

email: jack.bloggs@ABC.uk.com

High performance tips

- Send the agenda to the prospect prior to the meeting so they are clear on exactly why you are coming to see them and what you're looking to come away with. It also gives them time to establish their objectives and make them clear to you.

- You will get a lot more from the meeting if you do this and it often brings to the surface who else might need to be involved from the prospect or supplier side, to answer all points on the agenda.

- Use an agenda to manage expectations. If you offer an agenda to the client they might respond with something you weren't expecting. This can help qualify the meeting as there is no point in having one if what they expect on the agenda is something that you can't deliver, or vice versa – they have no need for what you have to offer.

● Sometimes an agenda will flush out the fact that the meeting should happen in a few months rather than now, so time expectations are also managed properly.

● Once in the meeting, use the agenda to recap the objective, ask if anything has changed and agree the length of the meeting.

5 Rapport

Most sales people have strong rapport as it is one of the more natural aspects related to sales. However, there is a big difference between rapport done badly, with no attentiveness, and well used rapport.

There is a plethora of books and digital downloads purporting to be able to help build rapport and interpret body language. But isn't this easy anyway? Body language is simple, right? Don't crossed arms mean closed off? Be careful not to fall into the trap of superficial psychology. You may find yourself in a pit of quick sand and sink faster than you thought possible.

Pitfalls

● **No conversation**. It is remarkable the number of sales people I have met that say very little when they meet the prospect for the first time and are obviously uptight and nervous or anxious. This will put the prospect on edge and they will immediately have a lack of confidence in you. You want them to be relaxed so they focus on what you're saying, their issues and the proposition you are going to make.

- **Straight into your offering**. Many sales people sit down and go straight into discussing their product or service with no other conversation. This is not a way to build rapport as the prospect will just feel spoken *at* and therefore quite distant from you as a person.

- **No interest**. It is human nature that if you show no interest in someone and what they do or are about, they will show little interest in you.

Getting the basics right is very important as first impressions can be hard (although not impossible) to change and you don't want to make your Critical Hour harder than it needs to be. Getting people to feel relaxed is important, so showing some inner confidence in yourself is essential.

It is important to make the prospect to feel at ease and for you to react to their mood. If they are in a hurry or short of time, then speed up and be succinct. If they are laid back and slow, then pace yourself accordingly.

High performance tips

- Don't be late for your meeting – always get there 15 minutes beforehand so you are relaxed when the prospect arrives or have time to set up if need be.

- Shake hands firmly with the client (not too hard though) and make sure you smile and look them in the eye when you do.

- Pick a topic to discuss, such as the weather, your journey, a recent major sporting event or if they live locally. Something that is easy to start dialogue so you can start to feel how open or closed they might be.

- Pass your business card to them, and when they give you theirs make sure you read it.

- Listen to what they have to say and show you are interested in it.

- Find something that they are interested in that you can discuss and ask questions about.

- Adjust the delivery of your presentation and discussion in line with the pace of the prospect.

6 Introductions

A lot of things in sales are straightforward but people forget to do them as they become nervous when they make a presentation. I am amazed how often people fail to introduce themselves and their colleagues, meaning that the other people in the room are a mystery to the customers. What a strange way to conduct a meeting and understand your audience. So always take the time to introduce or find out about all the people in the room. Good questions to ask when presenting to a group of people are:

> 'Could you tell me who you are, what you do, what you'd like to get out of this meeting? And if you could change one thing about … [whatever relates to your product or service] then what would it be?'

This gives you time to see each person speak, and find out what they want and what some of their pains are, which you will use later on. Make sure you write them down! Remember what we said about memory in Chapter 2 – it is a very fallible tool.

When you introduce yourself make sure you confirm your role and responsibilities, thank the prospect for the meeting and reconfirm its length and objectives. Then check that they agree or if they would like to add or change anything.

So you're now ready to start the main part of the meeting. Surprised at how much you've done so far? You'd be amazed at the number of people that don't do any of the above!

High performance tip

Take the time to introduce yourself and your colleagues and get your prospect to explain what they do and their responsibilities.

---

7 Sales person's conduct

This aspect relates to how you behave throughout the whole length of your Critical Hour. You need to be on form throughout the meeting, not just at the beginning.

So continue to be warm, friendly, well-mannered, articulate and attentive, and smile where appropriate. Maintain eye contact and be passionate about your company and its products and services.

All of this continues to build rapport with the prospect and will help them warm to you as a person and build respect for you.

Be sure to take notes so you can reference them in the meeting if necessary, and at the end when you recap on next steps. You'll be surprised what you can miss if you don't write things down. When it comes to writing a proposal later on those notes will prove invaluable if you have a short-term memory like mine.

> **High performance tip**
> Remember you are being assessed by your prospect throughout the whole meeting so ensure you are attentive, happy, enthusiastic, passionate and well-mannered throughout.

8 Meeting management

It is essential that you keep an eye on the time. You don't want to get to the end of the meeting and find you've not finished your presentation or left time for questions and next steps at the end. This happens all too frequently and is down to poor meeting management.

By agreeing objectives and the time the client has allowed you at the start of the meeting, you should be able to keep it on track.

Pitfalls

Don't be taken 'off piste'

- You will find that people you are presenting to will take you away from the main thrust of your presentation. They usually don't do this deliberately (although some do) but they start to ask questions that move on to a side topic related to what you are discussing. Before you know it you have completely moved away from the path of your pitch and lost a lot of time talking about something irrelevant to your end goal.

- Watch out for these people, especially when presenting to a group, as some use the opportunity to show off to their peers or bosses and take the whole meeting off track.

Don't lose track of time

- Remember the world we live in. Most people are very busy and only have a set amount of time to meet you and listen to what you have to say. Whether they like you and what you're offering or not, they have another meeting to go to or things to do. As interesting as you are, they do not have all the time in the world to listen to you.

- If you run out of time, getting another meeting in the diary with important people will take a long while to rearrange, if they do it at all. So make sure you get to the point and conclusion in good time for a discussion at the end about next steps.

- Don't labour points unnecessarily and don't get lost in your world – remember it's all about them, not you!
- If you have prepared properly for the meeting and agreed an agenda with the prospect, then stick to it or you will look unprofessional and the prospect will be confused as to where the meeting is going.

Don't do all the talking
- The prospect wants to know that you understand their business, so listen to what *they* have to say and ask open questions. If you do all the talking then the likelihood is they won't buy from you.

I had an account manager working for me who had no concept of time and had an incredibly high attention to detail. We were in a meeting with three very senior directors of a client of ours and had been given 90 minutes for the meeting. One was an advocate, one knew about the work we had been doing with them but needed to buy into the next stage, and the other was new and had no idea who we were. So this was going to be difficult as there were very different levels of knowledge about our approach in the room.

They all wanted to understand why they should continue to work with us, what we would recommend as a way forward and outline costs/ROI.

So what should have happened is this:

Prior to the meeting the account manager should have tried to get a quick WebEx meeting with the new person so they could be brought up to the same level of knowledge about us as the others in the room. Also it would have been a chance to do an early sales job on them.

As that didn't happen we should have recapped on previous work for 15 minutes at the start, then gone into the success of that programme (highlighting ROI), demonstrated our way forward (which we had spent four weeks working on to present to them), discussed value and ROI and then allowed time for questions and a close to next steps.

This is what happened:

The director who was new turned up 15 minutes late, so putting even more pressure on the timing of the meeting. She apologised and it was agreed that in light of the time, the meeting should focus on the future and only spend a little time on the past.

My account manager then proceeded to explain the previous programme in immense detail for the next hour. As interesting as that was to the new person my account manager suddenly looked at her watch and realised it was 5.45pm. She had only 15 minutes left and had not discussed the future solution which is why we had all come to the meeting. She asked for a further 30 minutes, which she was granted.

We moved on to the future solution, but, rather than learning from her previous lack of time management, she proceeded to go into immense detail, leaving no time to discuss value or ROI.

At 6.45pm two of the directors said, 'Sorry, but I really have to get back home to my family so perhaps you can just send through a proposal and we'll have a read of it?'

What do you think they were thinking? Not only had the meeting been completely mismanaged and the objective they clearly laid out at the start not been achieved as a result, but their personal time had been compromised, which is always a real no-no. When things affect someone personally in a negative way that is what will stay with them more than anything else.

Suffice to say it took ages to get them round a table again, which delayed the deal (which we eventually won) by four months. Four months due to mismanagement of the meeting!

As a quick aside, there is often a big difference between new business people and their succinctness, and account managers who like to discuss the detail. Both have their place but both must be managed properly in terms of keeping to the point and timing in meetings.

High performance tips

Keep the meeting on track

- If you do have people in the room who try to take you 'off piste' then don't be afraid to say, 'Could we come back to that at the end?' or 'Do you mind if I speak to you about that after the meeting?' This is where your pre-agreed agenda becomes your friend and saviour as you can reference it, and the time allowed for the meeting, as a reason to bring the presentation back to the main point.

Keep the meeting on time

- Keep to time. Make sure you have rehearsed your

presentation and you know how long you are going to leave for questions at the start, presenting your solution in the middle and questions/next steps/closing at the end. It's advisable to keep up a good pace, being succinct throughout.

● Confirm the amount of time the clients have allowed for the meeting at the start and conduct your presentation accordingly.

Stick to the agenda

● If you have gone to the trouble (which you should, as it is best practice) in creating an agenda with the prospect, make sure you stick to it!

● Cover the prospect's objectives in the meeting and ensure they have been personally engaged throughout.

9 Specifying customer needs

Now we're into the really important part of your Critical Hour. Time to get your prospect talking – this and the next two sections are the most fundamentally important part of selling. It's where so many sales people fall down today, because they are so keen to speak about or demonstrate their product or services.

Pitfalls

● **Don't do all the talking**. Just think for a minute here. It's not about you, it's all about the prospect. What is it about them or their situation that will make them realise they really need your solution? How are you going to position what you do with them so they are compelled to buy from you? If you do all the talking and just talk at them you won't have a clue what their needs or pains are, what they might be looking for or what they might dislike intensely. This also comes across as very rude as it will be all about you. Prospects don't like this.

- **Don't do a product pitch**. This follows on from the above. Don't just sit down after saying hello and start pitching your product or service, as you will have no idea how to orientate it to the prospect(s) in the room.

- **Don't try and sell them something they will never be able to afford**. This is a very common mistake that sales people make. They go through their whole pitch without any idea of whether the prospect can afford what they are offering. Frequently at the end of the meeting they will agree to send the prospect a proposal and it is only when the prospect receives it they find out about the cost. You must establish if the customer can afford what you are offering them.

I have done a lot of role-plays in my time, either looking to recruit someone for my company or for a clients, or to assess someone's sales capability. Role-plays create a high-pressure situation and I enjoy them when they are done well.

However, so many are done very poorly. All too often I have had a person start presenting their product or service to me without asking me a single question. I let them go through it, nodding in the right place, and when they are finished and ask me if I'd like to buy it, I tell them that I am not the right person they should be speaking to and if I were, I don't see a need for what they are selling. This highlights to them that they didn't even start at first base by confirming I was the right person to speak to and then finding out what *my* needs were. Failed immediately.

You need to get the prospect compelled to want to buy from you. Do that well and you'll not even get round to *having* to close them. They will be asking you when they can have your solution!

High performance tips

Find out what the prospect think their needs are

- Your initial open questions are there to establish what the client's needs are relating to your products or services. You are looking to understand what's on their mind and what solutions they may be thinking of. So you need to open the prospect up and get them talking about their needs in relation to what you do.

- You also need to establish why they think they have those needs. The *why* is very important as it gives you the thread for the next section – understanding challenges and pains.

Find out who the competition is

- If they are coming up with needs, use this opportunity to see if they are speaking to competitors or how they think those competitors might fulfil their needs.

- Also remember that the competition can be internal, within your prospect's company. So find out what the stoppers, accelerators or politics could be in their company that could influence their needs.

- Doing nothing is also an option. What is the cost to

---

them of doing nothing and is it an option they would consider?

Find out if they have a budget

● It is essential to understand if there is a budget for what you are offering. If there isn't, then find out what is needed to get one, when their financial year starts, or if their business allows for special cases to be made for solutions that will benefit the organisation.

● There is no point in trying to sell someone something they will never be able to pay for. You'll save a lot of time by identifying this upfront.

● Also establish when they can spend that budget. Some companies issue a budget but then freeze expenditure in a particular quarter. This will also give you an indicator on how the company is doing if that is the case.

● Just as an aside, if you sell in Spain then don't ask this question. It is an insult and the meeting will end very quickly. This highlights an additional layer of learning needed to understand different cultures when selling abroad.

Find out who is in the decision making unit (DMU)

● Always remember that it is very unlikely that the person you are selling to is the sole decision maker (I talk about different types of buyers later). Normally there will more than one person making the decision, so it is good to understand who they might be at this stage. You then know if you have to sell to more than just the person in front of you at a later stage.

● If you have built a good rapport with your prospect

and they are really interested in what you are selling (see building a champion under 'Personal pains' later in this section), they will help you to understand what the motivators, needs and pains are of the others in the DMU.

- If the prospect can list all their needs then you know that they are ready to buy from someone. If they can't, then there is work to do to create a business case, and more meetings to involve the right people. You need to keep all this information for the closing steps of your Critical Hour.

10 Understanding challenges/pains

Whether you have uncovered the prospect's needs in the section above or not, you need to find out what the pain is that is causing the need. You need to know the simple cause and effect and the measurable impact that this pain is having: I have a pain; therefore to take it away I need X.

Pitfalls

- **Don't stop at needs**. Many times a prospect has told me they need something. However, by clever questioning using open questions I have uncovered a pain that they were not even aware they had, and in fact they needed something completely different which was far more effective.

- **Don't ask closed questions**. Asking a question that can only be answered yes or no will not enable a prospect

> to discuss things openly. It is when a person starts discussing what's going on in their world that you can get to understand how they are feeling and what their potential pains could be.

By understanding pains, you get to the power play in selling. If you can uncover pains the prospect was not aware of and you can resolve them, you start to become a trusted adviser – the highest level of sales person you can aspire to. The prospect will start to listen to you in a new way and will see you in a different light to that of a sales person.

The key to the above is using open questions, which is something sales people often find hard to do.

So what is an open question and why is it important to be expert in their use when selling? The answer to this is covered in section 11 below, under 'Listening and questioning'.

To be able to search for pain you need to know what the difference is between a pain and a need.

Let me give you an example.

I have a blinding headache which keeps coming back week after week. My traditional sales person sells me some paracetamol and it goes away temporarily but returns with vengeance a few days later. They keep selling me the paracetamol as that is what they think I need. They *tell* me, 'You need paracetamol – that will get rid of your headache.'

However someone who is better at selling comes along and asks me some open questions. 'What is causing the headaches? How long have you had them?'

I discover that the cause is the stress in my neck and what I need is acupuncture, massage, to change my diet and do some exercise. So by looking to understand the pain and its causes I am given a completely different solution.

Do you think I am worried about the cost of taking the pain away? No, I just want the pain removed at any cost.

So by searching for pains and their causes you can often highlight to the prospect new solutions they hadn't thought of for which they will be very appreciative. Price can often go out of the window at this point – you have just delivered real value.

When uncovering pains, look to understand whether they are tactical or strategic and ask the prospect to estimate the financial impact they are having on their business. Strategic pains will normally be more costly and time-consuming to change and remove but also have a longer-term positive impact if you do.

Here's another example.

The issue is that my sales people need to improve their skill set and sales capability so they close their pipeline and increase their revenues. My pain is that they are not selling properly.

So the normal tactical thing to do is to put them on to a training course for two to three days. The problem with that is that the course will not change behaviour unless the sales manager attends it with the sales people and then coaches each member of their team in the new skill set thereafter. However, my managers don't know how to coach properly.

So the strategic pain is I need to create a coaching culture and to do that all layers of sales management have to become coaches. That is a longer-term goal and a larger investment of time and money. However, once they are able coaches, then they will be sustaining learning way into the future on an ongoing basis, which will have a real, positive impact on my revenue growth.

Also check to see if the pains are slowing anything down or hindering growth or positive change. All this, together with the tactical versus strategic pains, can be quantified, so the prospect starts to see the cost of doing nothing – one of your biggest and often invisible competitors!

Nothing is better at focusing the mind than working out the cost of doing nothing or what the cost of a pain is on clients' business. Numbers are how businesses are measured and how ROI calculations are created. If you can show how you can improve ROI in this day and age you will have the attention of the board and the possibility of a sale.

Highlighting all this to the prospect will enable them to start to think there is a need to take these pains away. It will also start to create a sense of urgency and a sense of value in working with you.

UNCOVERING PAINS

Every company will have a set of common reasons why people buy their products. If you expand that thought process to create the common pains your clients or prospects have that your products or services take away, then you can start to create a toolkit that sales people can use and a reason for customers to buy from you.

For example, let's take a company that sells customer relationship management software. What they are actually selling is a piece of software that stores all the information about your customers and prospects.

A **transactional** sales person will sell the features, benefits and cost of their software versus those of a competitor. For example, a feature may be the ease of use, the way in which you can integrate marketing campaigns or how a number of people can work on a client together and share information.

The benefits are that more people will use it, you can track calls made and meetings that happen off the back of a campaign to measure its effectiveness, and you get people to collaborate on one account, recording all the information in one place. Transactional sales people only discuss the product and its functionality and push that.

A **consultative** sales person, who is looking to understand pains, will take a different approach and will ask a host of open questions to uncover their real pains.

Through their questions they might find that:

- The clients have real problems keeping track of all the information that a new business person has on a prospect, which gets lost when an account manager takes over the account. So they have had a number of complaints from clients about the lack of knowledge shown by their account manager. One client gave the initial order but was so unimpressed that they did not order anything more and moved their account to a competitor. The lost revenue was worth £45,000.

- The sales director is hugely frustrated that they are not able to track the activity rates of their sales force to see how many calls are being made that are then converting to appointments. Then how many meetings are attended each week and of those, how many convert to sales. This lack of information is affecting their ability to manage the team properly as they do not have the facts to hand.

- The CEO and operations director are furious with the sales director because the Excel spreadsheet that they get each month forecasting the next six months' revenue is always far too optimistic and never accurate. Sales people are filling it in optimistically because the sales director has given them a KPI about the amount of pipeline they need to show each month. This is affecting the scheduling of work in operations and is causing the company to order too much raw material, which is mounting up in the warehouse and has not been sold. This is turn is affecting their balance sheet negatively to the tune of £500,000.

So two very different approaches that reveal very different information and results.

The **consultative** sales person will now be able to create a very compelling proposition around the pains that have been revealed. They will be able to solve all three pains above with their CRM software and can state the financial impact it will make due to:

- No loss of clients, with a smooth transition from new business to account management.
- Instant statistics about activity, enabling the sales director to motivate the team and ensure a higher level of productivity.
- Accurate pipeline forecasting, leading to correct levels of stocks in operations and improving the £500,000 impact on the balance sheet.

The product or **transactional** sales person has only demonstrated better features and their related benefits.

When it comes to the cost discussions, who do you think is going to discount and end up competing on price? Yes, the product guy every time. The consultative sales person will maintain their margins and will have cemented themselves firmly as the supplier of choice with the executive team. Job done!

One of the most important things for any company to do is to spend a day together as a senior management team and work this out. You will identify a suite of different pains, which is going to be used in creating sales value propositions later on.

PERSONAL PAINS

Everything described above relates to company pains. However, an individual can also have personal pains and if they think you can remove them too then they will be compelled to buy from you.

For example, the person you're selling to may be spending a lot of time in the office after work, due to the inefficiency of the systems their company deploys. They don't see their children after work until the weekend and that is really upsetting them. If your system meant they could leave at 6pm, how much will that person want to get your solution into their company?

So you also need to search for personal pains as well as corporate ones.

In doing this you can start to create a 'champion' within the prospect's company. A champion is a person that will do the selling on the inside for you. What is crucial when you create one is that they can articulate your proposition as well as you can to their colleagues. Maybe with even more passion.

All too often sales people create champions but do nothing to help them with the internal sales process or teach them how to position and describe what they do. So a well-articulated, concise and easy-to-understand value proposition goes a long way to help champions internally sell your offering.

So with the example above of the CRM software you would give your 'champion' the proposition around:

- Smooth transition between new business and account management, ensuring happy clients who spend more.
- A well-managed, motivated and more productive sales force due to accurate data provided to the sales director.
- No excess stock in the warehouse and accurate pipeline forecasting, creating efficient operations.

That is a very different set of compelling propositions that the champion can use, in contrast to the ones on the corporate brochure of the CRM company that will be generic and won't stand out when considered alongside other competitive offerings.

The champion can now get actively selling for you and will be excited to do so as it will raise their profile inside their organisation.

BUILDING RELATIONSHIPS

Once you understand a client's pains, you can build relationships with them. The main relationships are:

- **Tactical:** The sales person is only interested in supplying the client with the products or service they need. If they need something, they provide it; if they don't, they don't push the relationship any further.

- **Consultative:** The sales person uses their questioning and listening skills to really work out the right solution for the client. They have worked out what the client's pains are and by working with the client they work out how to remove them, utilising the sales persons offering.

- **Trusted adviser:** The client will ask the sales person their advice and the sales person will work out what the best solution is for the client, even if sometimes that involves buying products or services that they cannot provide. The sales person is firmly entrenched in the psyche of the client and should that person move to another company, they will work with the sales person there too.

Here is a real-life example we had with one of our clients who was selling food products to chains of restaurants.

The tactical sales person was in a meeting with a client who wanted to buy 10 tonnes of rice. The sales person offered the price and the client asked for a lower price. There ensued a tennis match where the sales person would drop the price slightly and the client would raise theirs by a small amount. They went backwards and forwards until they settled somewhere in the middle and shook on a deal. The sales person left happy, as he had sold 10 tonnes of rice with a small profit margin. His target was based on total volume of sales rather than profit margin, so he didn't care about achieving anything else.

After training the sales person in consultative sales, we sent him back to that client a few months later. The first thing he did when the client wanted to repeat the order was to question him.

'Why do you want so much rice?'

'Because that's what we sell the most of.'

'Why don't you sell more chips?'

'They are not popular in our restaurants.'

With continued questioning the sales person discovered that the quality of the chips they had been buying from a competitor was very low indeed and so absorbed a lot of oil, making them greasy to touch and taste. He also discovered that the quality of the deep-frying oil was also low and so they were ordering far too much.

By discussing this with the client he was able to offer better quality chips and oil (as a trial) as they were far more profitable than rice. Through the better quality products, the restaurant started to sell more chips, so they made more money as a result.

Building on the consultative approach, the now trusted adviser wanted to get a deeper understanding of how things worked in kitchens. So he went to see a number of chefs in a few of their restaurants and asked them some questions.

In doing so he discovered that the amount of low quality oil they were ordering was becoming onerous in terms of storage space in the kitchens and that one chef had had one of the sous chefs fall over a barrel and break their wrist. He was now suing the company. So Health and Safety had been compromised, which was a much bigger issue than just the quality of chips and oil.

He also did his research on the type of friers they were using and found out they were 20 years old and so were terribly inefficient. The trusted adviser's company also provided kitchen equipment.

So the adviser wrote a report and went back to present it to the main buyer and the finance director. As a result he walked away with a frier leasing deal for £500,000 a year for five years, as well as the order for chips, oil and rice (maintaining a higher margin than when he was tactically selling). The client was delighted as this increased their profit considerably and gave them far more efficiency and space in the kitchens. That made the staff happier as a result and customers came back more frequently because of the improved quality of the food.

And this all started because the adviser asked one question: 'Why do you want so much rice?'

High performance tips

- Use open questions to establish the customer's pains.
- Establish whether their pain is tactical or strategic.
- Is the pain slowing or hindering growth, or does it have a positive connotation?
- Quantify the cost of the pain to the business if it is not removed, and highlight this to the prospect.
- Quantify the ROI if it is removed, and highlight that to the prospect.
- Take a consultative sales approach and work your way to becoming a trusted adviser.
- Find and create your champion.
- Look for the personal pains of the prospect as well as the company ones.

11 Listening and questioning

Listening and questioning is an essential part of the sales cycle and sales meeting. It seems bizarre that time and book space should be dedicated to such a fundamental skill. After all, from the moment we master communication from a very early age, we have been listening and asking questions, right?

Although the young child may not have the linguistic sophistication of an adult, what they do have is the ability to ask questions, over and over again, until they get an answer with which they are satisfied. As we grow older and mature, we learn to conform to social norms. These are the behaviours we need to adopt in order to fit in with what is acceptable in society. For example, how odd would it look if an adult were to throw a tantrum in a supermarket because their partner would not get them a bag of sweets? A very tempting concept!

Conforming to social norms can take away some of the natural curiosity of a young child. In fact, they often display some key attributes of great sales people. Anyone who has had children will have witnessed them at some stage asking mum for a treat. Upon hearing the answer 'no' the child is not perturbed. They know that they need to go and ask someone else. In this case dad. Will they get a different result? Who knows, but at least they are aware of the key influencers in this relationship.

Children are also good at trying for the direct close as well. They are not afraid of asking the question 'Can I have …' The lack of sophistication that they have in communication then descends in to a series of challenges, i.e. overuse of the word 'why'. As sales professionals, we can learn a lot from children in their navigation around relationships to get what they want. As adults we learn the linguistic sophistication, but can be victims of the thief of curiosity.

Without curiosity, we do not manage to find out any information. Curiosity is fuelled by great questioning. Great questioning is having the ability to ask the right question at the right time. Within this section, we explore the key areas and types of questions that are used and discuss their effectiveness and, conversely, their destructiveness.

QUESTIONING

Closed questioning
Closed questions are those that simply demand a 'yes' or 'no' answer, or a sharing of facts demanded of the question. For example: 'How are you?' 'Where do you live?' 'Are you coming to the coffee shop?' They are valuable in their own right. They can be used to set the right frame of mind.

Asking a closed question can help to gain a commitment one way or the other; they can be a way of introducing persuasion. Closed questions are quick and easy to answer. In a sales meeting situation, closed questions should be used to close, pre-close or ensure clarification of understanding of the information shared.

Using closed questions for clarification is essential to ensure that all parties are in agreement and still on the same page. Without such an exercise it is quite possible for both parties to go off at tangents through misunderstanding of meaning. Before you know it, you are miles apart and the assumption culture is prevailing.

Imagine two ships leaving port for the same destination, but their compasses are out by just one degree of calibration. Within a few miles of leaving they are a little way apart. By the time a few hours have passed, they are miles apart from each other and out of sight.

Open questioning

Open questions are the best tool we have for gaining information. They are driven by the big six curiosity words:

1 Who?
2 What?
3 Where?
4 Why?
5 When?
6 How?

Starting a question with these words will encourage the other party to respond with a fuller answer than for a closed question. It forces them to think about their answer or reflect, and it encourages them to consider whether they will share opinions, feelings or thought processes. One of the most important aspects of asking open questions is that it places the emphasis and responsibility to answer on the other party.

This method is one of the most important and powerful ways for you to open up the customer and get to learn about what they are thinking and what their concerns are. Too few sales people use this approach and so end up making huge assumptions about what they think the customer needs and when they need it.

Something else I have observed when working with many sales managers, sales leaders, MDs, commercial directors and the like is how few use open questions when 'coaching' their sales staff or managers.

In fact, few sales managers really understand what coaching is and usually think that a weekly or monthly one-to-one with their team member, where they discuss pipeline, client issues or internal issues, constitutes a coaching session. Wrong!

The questions tend to be closed rather than open and the nature of the conversation errs towards a directive one, where the manager tells the sales person or manager what they should do, rather than using open questions to get them to learn and think for themselves about what the best course of action could be.

Leading questions

Leading questions are those that plant seeds of direction in the recipient. In a sales situation they can be extremely valuable. It is possible to incorporate leading questions into open questions for added effect. Leading questions help the other party to consider issues that are important to you. That is not to say that using such questioning is Machiavellian, it simply gives you the opportunity to interject an angle that maybe the other party had not thought of, or is not considering, in their deliberations.

Let's imagine you are selling an insurance product and the other party is not considering what you think are the key pains. Your open questioning may be along the lines of:

'What is the reason you buy insurance at the moment?'

'How do you currently decide on what policy to buy?'

These questions, as discussed above, are going to get the other person thinking and they are likely (assuming they are happy to talk) to result in you getting plenty of good information back.

Consider an alternative approach by using a leading question.

'What are the personal dangers to you if you do not buy insurance?'

This is similar to the open question above, with a subtle introduction of our own interpretation of not buying insurance. In the leading question we are suggesting, albeit subtly, that they consider that not buying insurance is dangerous. Moreover, that it is dangerous to them personally (which is what we may believe). With a subtle change of emphasis in the questions used, we are able to have the other person consider different angles and allow ourselves to magnify the pain that is now in focus.

Layered questions

Layered questions are used a lot in everyday conversation. They are somewhat stealth-like in that they creep into conversation mostly without us knowing. Layered questions can occur due to high activity in the working brain. In a sales situation this may be when we are getting excited by the idea of closing the deal.

In fact there are always a lot of things going on in our minds, possibly more than we can process at any one time. Working memory has a limited capacity or about seven items of information and a very limited timespan of less than 20 seconds before things fade. Due to this fallibility, there is a temptation to just spill our thoughts out and place the emphasis on the other person.

For example, you are in a meeting and sense that it is going really well. You have identified a number of different ways in which your solution can be used by the customer, and even identified some areas that they have not even begun to think about. You are in a heightened state and just want to ask a heap of questions, but which one? In reality it may come across like this:

> 'Would you say that the best thing to concentrate on is the production model, or would it be better to look at the manufacturing issue, or how about if we look at the customer service problem and sales system? What else do you think would be best?'

In the above example, the sales person has asked four questions. Which one do you think would be answered? This can depend on a number of factors. If the recipient is a primacy driven person, then they are likely to remember the first thing they heard and forget the rest. If they are a recency-driven person, they are likely to remember the last question asked.

Chances are they will not remember all of the questions asked. And here is the danger. It is unlikely that as the deliverer of the message you will remember all of the questions you asked, so you will be more likely go with the answer you get and shoot along that line of enquiry.

So what was the purpose of asking so many questions and not checking for the results? In the above example, each question appears to be as valid as the next. How do we know that the most important question has not been answered?

It is not just an overly active mind that causes us to ask layered questions. The opposite of the overly active mind is the latent mind. In such cases, there is a lack of real punch and activity going on. The synapses are not firing so quickly and you may find it hard to know where to go next with your line of enquiry.

You can often spot this in a conversation. It manifests itself as a scattergun approach to questioning, but this time, instead of being delivered at pace as in the above example, the delivery is more laboured and often the questions will either be repeated, or be the same thing just reframed. For example:

'Is it fair to say that you need to do something differently, or should you change what you are doing? What else do you think you should do?'

Using layered questions can lead to confusion and a lack of quality information for you to gather. It is important to ensure that questioning has purpose and is not just something we do to fill the empty space of silence between two parties. Without purpose and direction, questioning is an empty exercise and therefore a waste of time.

Learning how to question

Taking into account all that has been stated above, do not despair. Even the best and most highly trained interviewers still get it wrong. Next time you look at a programme where an interviewer, journalist, broadcaster or chat show host is on the television, listen carefully to what they are saying. Taking into account everything considered on the subject of questioning, you will be surprised at just how patchy this skill is, even among those that are highly trained.

You may see this in evidence a lot in interviews with politicians. Commonly, closed questions are used. Luckily for the interviewer, the politicians indulge them with a full answer, but they have every right just to say 'yes' or 'no'.

Such poor questioning was outlined recently by a friend, who was trying to have a conversation with their 14-year-old son via text. He was asking questions, but only getting one-word answers back. After a few attempts to find out information, he texted his son and said, 'Why won't you just tell me the answer?', to which his son said, 'Because you keep asking just closed questions'. A lesson learnt there.

Buyer and seller questions

Thinking about all that has been discussed above about different types of questioning, we still need to explore another aspect: the focus and angle with which we come at the questions.

Let's consider some of the usual questions that are asked in typical sales calls. During my years of managing sales people and speaking to my trainers I have found this to be a consistent issue. For example, we have looked at what questions are asked in a sales meeting and we find these are the most common:

What is the budget?
Who is the decision maker?
What are your timeframes?
How is your business performing?
Who are you using at the moment?
Who else are you talking to?
When is your year end?
How many people have you got working for you?
Can you tell me why you asked me to meet you?

Sometimes there is a change of emphasis in questioning, which makes a huge difference to how you are perceived as a sales person. If we consider that the above questioning is somewhat typical, then buyers will hear these questions all day long from multiple different sales people. At the end of the day, they cannot distinguish one sales person from another.

It is like having a star being interviewed by a multitude of different journalists in one day to promote their new film. If you analyse these interviews, you will discover that the line of questioning will largely follow the same theme, i.e. 'What was it like on set?' 'How much fun did you have during filming?', etc. The ones that are remembered are those that did something different.

This skill is available to you and within your power to enact at any time you wish. Take another look at the questions above. Think about what they are seeking to do. Is there anything you can identify from that line of questioning that has a theme?

All the questions above are seller questions. That means that they are focused on getting information for the benefit of the seller. The other party in this instance (the buyer) already knows the answer to these questions, so the only person that really benefits from these questions is the seller.

Let's suppose that the bulk of your sales meeting was spent asking seller questions. As a seller, you would walk away with a lot of useful information, but how much further have you advanced the sale? What else has your buyer learnt about you? How much have you made them think?

Buyer questions, by contrast, are those great questions that get the buyer thinking hard about how to answer. It may even be in an area that they have not given any or much consideration to in the past.

When I was working with a financial institution, just such an exercise was conducted with the sales people. After talking about the difference between buyer and seller questions, attention was turned to getting a good list of buyer questions together to use in sales meetings in the future.

A number of the sales people were suggesting that their clients did not require financing because they had all the equipment they needed. At this point, one delegate came up with a real killer buyer question:

'If I was just to give you £50,000 as a gift right now, what would you do with it?'

Having used this in a real-life situation, the delegate reported back that their client suddenly started to think of all the possibilities and what they could do with £50,000.

Great buyer questions are the golden treasure for sales people. You will know when you have asked one, because the buyer will often go quiet for a moment as they consider their response. At this point they may either verbalise 'That's a good question' or be thinking it. Allow the time to bask in your skill and keep the silence. Breaking it will break the buyer's thought process. Give them space and time to formulate a considered response.

Not only will asking great buyer questions differentiate you from the competition, but it will also allow you to be remembered and your newly probed focus will stay at the forefront of the buyer's mind.

Think how powerful that would be if you have got the buyer thinking about a key issue that is then considered to be important, and it is in an area where you have a strong USP. Chances are your buyer will probe other suppliers around how they can help in this area. Guess what happens next?

It is important to have a kitbag of good quality 'get the buyer thinking' buyer questions.

Take a few moments to write down a list of great buyer questions. Maybe bring this up as a topic for brainstorming at your next sales team meeting, so the whole team can benefit from this powerful questioning emphasis.

High performance tips
Closed questions
- Use these to gain commitment, closure or clarification of understanding during your Critical Hour.

Open questions

● Use this approach to open up the customer and get to learn about what they are thinking and what their concerns are.

● Open questions always start with 'How?', 'Who?', 'What?', 'Where?', 'Why?' or 'When?'

Leading questions

● Leading questions help the other party to consider issues that are important to them.

● A change of emphasis on the questions used enables the other person to consider different angles and allows you to magnify the pain that is now in focus.

Layered questions

● This is where you ask many questions in the same sentence. Using layered questions can lead to confusion and a lack of quality information for you to gather.

● It is important to ensure that your questioning has purpose and is not just something we do to fill the silence between two parties.

Buyer and seller questions

● Seller questions are the ones you ask to help you with information *you* want.

● Buyer questions are those great questions that get the buyer thinking and will differentiate you in their mind from every other sales person they see asking seller questions.

● When you ask a buyer question, the buyer will go quiet so they can consider the answer. Allow them that time and do not break the silence.

LISTENING

Passive listening

Passive listening is defined as listening without reacting. This is the skill we use mainly when we are in the listening and questioning phase of the Critical Hour meeting. In its true sense, this is about not reacting to the conversation. However, this can quickly lead to an uncomfortable situation, as the other person may not feel as though you are fully engaged. Passive listening is allowing time for someone to speak without interrupting. It is allowing yourself the time to gather data, to get as much information about the situation as you can. Having this information will only serve you well in the later stages of the Critical Hour, as you will have so much more knowledge to draw upon.

This may sound an easy concept in theory, but take time out in your next meeting to understand your impulses. How often do you feel like you want to step in with comments and suggestions? It is easy for us to jump in and start asking questions and contribute to the conversation, and lead it on to our agenda without really realising it. Without passive listening, we may also fall into the layered questioning trap discussed above.

Passive listening is also about being there for the audience, giving your full attention to the situation and conversation. Although, as stated, it is about not reacting, it still does need some interaction from you, but this is mainly focused on keeping the conversation going in the right direction. Such interaction may be as simple as asking probing questions, or asking for fuller explanations of areas discussed if you do not fully understand.

Active listening

Active listening is the opposite of passive listening. It demands that you react and get involved in the conversation.

It is about demonstrating that you are listening and have understood.

There are a number of ways in which we can show that we are actively listening and some of these do not even need us to utter a word. Such instances can be non-verbal cues, such as nodding, making eye contact, facial expressions or smiling, all of which are appropriate to the situation and what has been said.

In addition to the non-verbal cues, we can also demonstrate that we are actively listening through small non-word verbal utterances. These tend to be the 'uhuh' and 'uhum' noises of affirmation as the conversation unwinds.

In active listening, we also reflect back the main points of the conversation. We do this at regular intervals to ensure that we can summarise and clarify what we have heard. This is clearly important to us in the Critical Hour to ensure that we are all still on the same wavelength. The easiest way to do this and also to help build rapport is to paraphrase and play back the conversation in the words and language of the other person. At a lower level of consciousness we find this confirms that we really are important in the conversation.

Empathic listening

Empathic listening is all about paying attention to the way in which the other person is talking. Up to now we have been talking about listening to the content of the conversations, but how boring they would be if they did not have any emotion in them. Empathic listening requires you to attend to the different clues that are given in the delivery of the message. It is not an exact science, but it can serve as a guide to us as to the mood or engagement of the other person.

To be good at this, we would really need to get some kind of baseline measurement of the other person's natural state. For example, in their natural state, someone's conversation may be somewhat slow and deliberate in delivery. By asking them about a subject they are passionate about (e.g. a hobby), you may be able to detect a change in their delivery style. When we know what they are like in an altered state, we can detect it more easily in our sales calls. We can spot when we are hitting the right notes. So, those long walks from the reception area to the meeting room can be valuable sources of benchmarking for us.

The variances here can be:

- **Pitch/ tone**. How high or low the voice of the other person is.
- **Pace**. How quickly they are talking. The faster they talk, the more interested they will be in the conversation.
- **Cadence**. The rhythm of their speech.
- **Intonation**. Do they inflect certain words or phrases? Is there any lift in their conversational delivery?

Empathic listening can also take into account the body language on show. A word of caution here about body language. There are a number of people that will understand that crossed arms = closed off. Crossed arms and crossed legs = well, you might as well leave the meeting now. This just is not the case. Body language is provided to us to give us clues. There is no hard science around this.

We need to work hard to detect the right signs. In a cold room, someone may have their arms closed to keep warm. It could simply be that they find it comfortable. In isolation, body language tells us only part of the story. We need to tie it up with the words being delivered and the *way* they are being delivered. We are looking for a level of congruence among all these factors.

For example, if you are in a conversation where the message is in line with what you expect to hear back from your questioning, the answers are full, pacey with rhythm and melody (not monotone) *and* you can detect that the other person has an open gesture, you know pretty much that you are well on the right path to a great interaction. Everything reconciles behaviourally.

A few years ago a friend was in Denmark selling some financial software to a financial institution. This was a highly technical meeting, so the sales guy took along a technical expert to discuss the finer detail. The sales guy had been sitting there for a good 30 minutes not really understanding the situation, or much of what they were even talking about. It was all too detail-focused for him. His mind had wandered on a number of occasions, until he had come back into consciousness of the meeting again, realising that maybe he should say something.

It was at this point that he piped up and said, 'I am really excited by this opportunity.' There was a lack of congruence of the message and his overall demeanour. This was picked up by the key influencer on the buyer side, whose reply was a damning, 'Well, maybe you should tell your face.' Needless to say, he did not get the deal.

High performance tips

Passive listening

● Passive listening is allowing time for someone to speak without interrupting. It is allowing yourself the time to gather data, to get as much information about the situation as you can.

● However, you need to interject from time to time so the prospect can see you are interested.

Active listening

● Active listening uses verbal and non-verbal cues to show you are listening and interested in what the other person is saying.

● It is also good to paraphrase what they have said and play it back to them so they know you have listened and understood. This also builds rapport.

Empathetic listening

● This is all about paying attention to the way in which the other person is talking. Listen out for:
  - Pitch/ tone: how high or low the voice of the other person is.
  - Pace: how quickly they are talking. The faster they talk, the more interested they will be in the conversation.
  - Cadence: the rhythm of their speech.
  - Intonation: do they inflect certain words or phrases? Is there any lift in their conversational delivery?

● If answers are full, pacey with rhythm and melody (not monotone) *and* you can detect that the other person has an open gesture, then you're on the right track.

12 Company background

Now you have a good understanding of what the client's needs and pains are, their budget, their timescales for resolution, who needs to be involved in making the decisions and other aspects described above, it is time to talk about *your* company.

Believe it or not I have seen so many presentations that start at this point. The sales person went straight into speaking all about themselves and their products and had literally done none of the above. You are going to have to have a pretty amazing product or service if you start here, and you're going to have to hope the prospect might be interested in it – pretty unlikely!

The company background is important so the prospect gets a sense of your pedigree, how long you've been in business, what you're about and what you stand for, and where you are going. This is the part where you start to build credibility so the prospect feels they are dealing with a reputable and reliable company.

> **High performance tip**
> Take the time to explain the history of your company so that you build credibility.

13 Positioning the company

This is a very important part of the Critical Hour. Many sales people miss the chance to really position their company in the prospect's mind. This is your chance to occupy a space in their thinking that no one else can own.

Here is one definition of positioning:

> *Positioning is a marketing strategy that aims to make a brand occupy a distinct position, relative to competing brands, in the mind of the customer. Companies apply this strategy either by emphasizing the distinguishing features of their brand (what it is, what it does and how, etc.) or they may try to create a suitable image (inexpensive or premium, utilitarian or luxurious, entry-level or high-end, etc.) through advertising. Once a brand is positioned, it is very difficult to reposition it without destroying its credibility. Also called product positioning.*

Several years ago Barclays ran an advertising campaign saying they were the 'really BIG bank'. At the time they were not the biggest bank in the UK or the world. They never had been.

However, anyone thinking, 'I want to open an account with the biggest bank' would naturally have thought of Barclays. So that way, for the time that campaign was running, Barclays owned the word 'big' in the consumers' mind. Barclays had positioned themselves as BIG.

Positioning differs from a value proposition in that the latter should be pain-related and always discuss the value (ROI) the customer will receive and what differentiates your company from the rest of the marketplace.

In contrast, positioning is how you want someone to remember you in the marketplace. It is the space you occupy in someone's mind, relevant to your offering.

Alongside positioning it is also good to mention your company strategy and vision, and possibly your brand values, which will also set you apart.

> **High performance tip**
> Make sure you position your company so the prospect will remember it distinctly.

14 Company offerings

So you have discussed your company background and have positioned your company firmly in the prospect's mind. Now you need to describe the products or services you offer that you think will be of interest and relevant to the prospect's needs and pains.

If you have a large portfolio then be sure to pick only the ones that you now know will interest the prospect. It is here that you should be doing the 'features' part of your Critical Hour.

So many people think selling is all about the features and benefits of your product offering but – as you can see from the structure of the Critical Hour – that represents only a tiny piece of the picture.

Be concise in the product description and, most importantly, move to the next section swiftly.

> **High Performance tip**
> Make sure you know your products and services inside out and be sure to describe the ones that are relevant to the prospect.

15 Matching customer pains to company offering

This is where the clever aspects of selling cut in and you start to hook your prospect.

Since you have done all the hard work in the Critical Hour properly up to this point, you will know exactly what products or services you need to be discussing with your prospect. Not only will you know which ones to demonstrate but you'll know exactly how they can benefit the client.

This is the benefits piece of the 'feature and benefit sell'.

However, generic benefits that you have been told to sell by your company don't always work. They have to be tailored to the prospect's pains, meaning you need to articulate how your products or service will take away their pain and how they will be better off by working with you as a result of using them.

Do this well, and the client will shift your way and become interested in what you have to offer and how you can help.

I used to sell online information for MAID (Market Analysis Information Database) in the 1990s. Interestingly, when I started in 1992, internet and email did not exist, mobile phones were in their infancy and laptops had just come out in their most basic form of a 286 (the memory size of early computers). That was only 20 years ago!

I needed to get online in order to demonstrate how we could enable a prospect's company to search for and download news and market research information directly on to their computer. The market research reports came from the likes of Mintel, Frost & Sullivan and Euromonitor. The overall report cost several hundred pounds but our system would enable the user to download just a page from the report that was relevant to their search. So you could do a search on a company and or industry and get some really powerful information.

The competition was fierce. We were only a tiny organisation turning over £6m going up against the might of the *Financial Times*, Dow Jones, Reuters, etc. We were pretty much all selling the same information – a news article from any of us about a company would be identical.

So MAID used technology and clever indexing of the data to differentiate itself.

In one meeting the prospect highlighted two things to me during the initial conversation where I was asking him about why he used information and the challenges he had in finding the right pieces.

First, he only wanted a few pages from a market research report and never had a need for the whole thing. He begrudged paying hundreds of pounds when he only used 5 per cent of the report.

Second, with online systems he had used in the past he never knew how much he had spent when he logged off. He would then have to wait for a month for the bill and this made managing his budget a nightmare. He had had several reprimands in the past for overuse of information (corporate and personal pain).

A product sales person might never have uncovered these facts, as they would simply have demonstrated the ability to get information online (a unique and unusual thing to do in the early 1990s) and then have gone for the close.

During the course of the demonstration I showed him how to retrieve just one page from a report. Then at the end of the demo I logged off and waited a minute (when I would have normally packed up and started to close without showing the log-out data) to show him how much we had spent in that session.

He had been fairly quiet and reserved during the demonstration but as soon as he saw the analysis of spend at the end he leapt around the fax machine ecstatically. *I had matched his pains to our offering.*

Due to the fact that I addressed his two main pains and showed how I could remove them, he was delighted and gave me the order, since I could help him not only manage his budget, but also spend less per search.

Through careful questioning I knew exactly what would excite and interest him and therefore help me seal the order.

This section has now set you up for the most important part of your Critical Hour – the sales value proposition.

16 Case studies

This is different to the use of anecdotes described later. This is where you take the customer through a much more detailed example of how you have worked with another company that was experiencing similar pains or problems to the ones the prospect has highlighted to you.

A case study is normally a two-page document (much longer than that and it is too long) that highlights the following:

● The original pain that the customer had and wanted to resolve.

● What your company provided to remove that pain.

● How long it took and what was involved.

- The end result in terms of ROI and other intangible benefits.
- A testimonial from the client.

It is therefore important to have a number of well-documented case studies that relate not just to your product or service offering, but also to the pains you removed and ROI that was gained as a result.

It goes back to understanding which categories of pain this client is in and retrieving the appropriate case study. This is why it is so important that sales work closely with marketing to ensure the sales force has the correct sales toolkit to use out in the field.

High performance tips

- When you describe the case study, keep relating the needs or pains you have already uncovered in your questioning to the case study, and how you helped your existing client to overcome them.

- This will build great confidence in your prospect that not only do other people have similar challenges, but also that you have helped resolve them and provided clear evidence of ROI.

- Importantly, don't spend too long on this part as you don't want to become a storyteller (see Chapter 1) and the meeting becomes all about your company and not enough about what the prospect needs.

- If the prospect is really interested and wants to learn about the case study in more detail then fine, but let them lead that discussion.

---

17 Sales value proposition (SVP)

The one thing a prospect needs to walk out of the room with at the end of your presentation is a clear understanding of the value proposition you have offered them. Not only does this need to stay in their mind, but it also needs to be straightforward enough for them to articulate it to others in their company.

A sales value proposition (SVP) needs to answer three questions:

1 Why should I buy your product or service?
2 Why should I buy from you? Why are you different?
3 What's in it for me? This means what is the ROI or what value am I going to receive?

Ultimately a SVP is a clearly differentiated statement of the tangible benefits a customer gets from using your products or services, giving you unique business value. It also forms the basis of your pitch to your customer, giving you a competitive advantage.

So a well-constructed SVP provides you with two powerful benefits:

1 A speedy but very effective way of communicating your unique business value and setting yourself apart from your competitors.
2 A simple but decisive way of defining your level of competitive advantage.

Everything I have described in the Critical Hour so far comes together here. At this point you should know from all the questioning and listening you have done exactly what pain 'bucket(s)' the prospects are in and which anecdote(s) to use.

Now let's understand about differentiation.

According to Tom Peters (in his *Manifestos 2002 – The Solutions Imperative: From 'Customer Satisfaction' to 'Customer Success'*):

> *'The world has a surplus of similar companies, employing similar people, with similar educational backgrounds, working in similar jobs, coming up with similar ideas, producing similar things, with similar prices and similar quality.'*

It's a fairly easy statement to understand, but how would you translate what Tom Peters is saying in your sales world?

We have to avoid the 'me too world of similarity' dialogue and craft a position of differentiation that motivates the customer to 'prefer' our solution.

SVPs are important because they:

- Communicate why a customer should buy from you.
- Create the interest, the value-based 'hook'.
- Define the ROI for the customer.
- Create a reason for decision makers and key influencers to see you.
- Set or change your company's image.
- Underpin long-term, value-based partnerships.
- Help to provide protection for prices and margins.
- Help to avoid pure commodity/price discussions.

TYPES OF SVP

SVPs are incredibly versatile in developing and building credibility and competitive advantage throughout a typical sales cycle. There are five main levels of SVP:

- Organisations need to communicate to their overall marketplace the value they deliver through their products and services. This high-level **company SVP** appears on company websites, in corporate brochures and press releases. They are frequently used by the marketing department but equally are very valuable as the starting point in the sales process when establishing initial credibility with a new prospect or contact.

- Early in the sales cycle, you may have very limited information about a target customer's business and even less information about a specific need and subsequent opportunity. This is where you can continue the process of building credibility, initiated by the company SVP, by demonstrating your value at the prospect's segment/ vertical level. For this purpose you would build a **segment SVP**. What are the key segments/verticals where you need to make a value-based impact?

- From the credibility created from your segment SVP, you can begin to gather specific information about the customer's business, its objectives and challenges. With this additional and more granular information, you can evolve your segment SVP into a much more focused **customer SVP**, building additional rapport and credibility with the key individuals as you do so.

- Once you have developed a customer-focused SVP, you can move on and pinpoint the specific business issue you believe you can address with your solution and start to craft an **opportunity SVP**. You may develop your opportunity SVP through a few iterations as you gather more detailed information from numerous key players.

- When, through the information-gathering process, you have identified the key players – decision makers and important influencers – then you can develop your opportunity SVP so that it focuses your unique business value on to the business and personal agendas of a specific key player – this is an **individual SVP**.

CREATING A COMPELLING SVP

The SVP structure looks like this:

- The customer's pain and its measurable impact.
- Your solution.
- Your differentiator(s).
- The measurable value (ROI) gained by the customer.
- Evidence – an anecdote of where you have solved a similar problem elsewhere.

Around 65 to 70 per cent of the actual content of an effective SVP will be customer focused! We also need an anecdote to reassure the customer of our ability to deliver what our SVP is promising.

What does that tell us about the role of SVPs in the sales process? To be compelling they have to be built and tailored from a sound base of information and insight about the customer issues you are addressing and the competitive environment.

So compelling SVPs are a function of how much you know about the environment in which you are operating. According to Donald Krause (in *The Art of War for Executives*):

'Information means getting facts – timely, accurate facts about the reality of conditions and circumstances in the competitive situation. Nothing in competition is more important than obtaining facts'

So what information do you need to know?

- The customer's business pain, its impact and cost.
- The competitive landscape for differentiation.
- The key players – decision makers/influencers.
- Our range of capabilities, which form our business solution.

This 'intelligence' becomes the raw material that we use to craft and tailor our SVPs. Harry Beckwith (in *Selling the Invisible*) defines a successful competitor as:

> *'Someone who is taking up more space in your prospect's brain than you are'.*

We are looking to capture mindshare with the key decision makers and influencers in the customer's organisation through well-crafted and tailored SVPs. It is vitally important that when they think about unique, measurable value, they only think about us!

A SVP should take *30 to 45 seconds* to read. We need to establish an effective position in the mind of the reader or listener and this is the timeframe with which we need to work. Any less than 30 seconds and the SVP will lack depth and credibility; any more than 45 seconds and we will run out of mindshare!

COMPETITOR RESEARCH

It's so important to be fully aware of your competitors, how they communicate their value and their USPs and points of differentiation. Once you have explored their approach and the language used, you are then in a better position to create a more dynamic and different proposition yourself.

When looking at a competitor's website, consider these points:

- Is there a clear message on the home page?
- What do you like about the message?
- What would you like to see more of in the message?
- What jargon or acronyms are used?
- Is there a clear ROI linked to people, product or money?
- What kind of language is used?
- Which words made an impact on you?

DIFFERENTIATION

Another issue that is important to remember for our SVP creation is that we need to find appropriate words that highlight our differentiators. The customer will not know that we are unique or different unless we state it clearly in the SVP.

Differentiation is a challenging issue, especially when our main focus is only on our products/services. So where else should we look for differentiation?

We need to stretch our thinking beyond just those items on the price-list and consider the full range of our capabilities. Here's a simple way of doing that:

- **Products/services**. Where are we different in terms of features, functionality or even price?
- **Process**. What aspects of our deployment, ongoing service, back-up etc. are unique?
- **People**. Where does the expertise and skill of our people set us apart from the competition?
- **Partners**. What alliances do we have that provide us with a unique cutting edge?

We also need to exercise care with how we introduce our USPs and differentiators into the sales conversation because we can simply 'offload' them on to the customer in the hope that they will be impressed. Relevance is critical here and we must tailor our differentiators to fit the specific sales situation or there will be minimal impact. Remember:

- Differentiators are of little or no value unless they connect with the client's business issues and needs.
- Differentiation is situational.
- Unique business value is the message you must convey.

High performance tips
- What's different about your **product/service**?
- What's unique about the **process**?
- How do your **people's** skills and expertise set you apart?
- Who are your **partners**, and why does that make a difference?
- What are your competitors' SVPs?
- Have you created the five different types of SVPs?
  - **i)** Company
  - **ii)** Segment
  - **iii)** Customer
  - **iv)** Opportunity
  - **v)** Individual

---

18 Anecdotes

An anecdote is a story about how a client has benefited from using your company's products or services. You should have a number of anecdotes that relate to different success stories and pains.

> **Pitfall**
>
> Don't forget your successes. Once you've done a presentation, always explain to the prospect how you have been successful with other clients and what you did to achieve that success for them.

Ask your happy clients to write testimonials for you – if you have taken the time out to identify the different common pains that your products or service remove (see the section on 'Understanding challenges and pains'), then this is where you need to tie in the client success stories that demonstrate to the prospect how you have worked with another organisation and successfully removed similar pains, providing a solution that delivered real ROI or value.

The number of sales people that don't use anecdotes always astounds me as it is such an important part of your Critical Hour and makes a huge difference to the success of the meeting. Prospects want to know how your solutions have worked for other companies and what your track record is, so tell them! It adds in a lot of credibility.

Every anecdote should have a testimonial from that client, a written statement from them stating how happy they are with you, and what a positive impact your solution has had on their business.

So what you end up with is a sales toolkit that can be used by you and across the sales force. Through your new questioning skills you can identify which category of pain the client is in and can quickly reference the correct anecdote and testimonial to demonstrate the value your company delivered.

If you are not sure of what anecdotes you have, then gather the sales and delivery team together and get them to describe some of the success stories they have experienced. You would be amazed at what sales people keep in their heads and never tell anyone. Make sure you capture all the detail properly and then go back to that client and ask for a written testimonial. When it comes to anecdotes, you don't need to have lived them personally, but they do need to be factual.

One important thing to point out is the use of stories can happen at any time in your Critical Hour and should happen throughout it. You need to think on your feet and, when the right moment arises, drop in an anecdote.

For example, here is an anecdote describing a sale I was involved in.

When we were asked to tender by BT Directories to take their 60 managers and turn them into world-class coaches, I said to the CEO that obviously the company that won that contract would turn them into decent coaches, but what would happen next?

He said, 'They will then go and teach their sales staff how to sell.'

I said, 'Yes, and will cascade bad practice brilliantly as they will teach them how to sell in *their* way of selling which will not be best practice. Instead, by combining coaching skills with the best practice data from our objective assessment approach, all 60 will coach their staff to a best practice standard.'

The result – 11 per cent growth in a year when the competition was failing to grow.

I would only use the anecdote above if I were speaking to someone about developing their managers and improving the capability of their frontline sales force. Using it I will highlight a number of things:

- We have already successfully transformed sales and coaching capability using the methodology I am demonstrating to this new prospect.
- We have successfully worked with a highly respected brand.
- We challenged the thinking of the CEO and he agreed with our rationale.
- The difference between our competitors offering and our approach.
- They had considerable ROI and financial gain as a result.
- They outperformed their competitors as a result.

FORMULATING ANECDOTES

Take a moment to think about some of the successes you have had while selling at your company and write down the following:

- What was the pain that your client had that you were able to remove?
- What did you do to remove it?

- What benefit or value did they gain as a result? For this think about not only financial gain but other intangible gains too.
- What did they say as a result of how pleased they were?

This will help you to formulate your anecdotes. Next – write them up into a testimonial and get the client to sign off on it for public use.

Remember, that although I have described anecdotes being related to a pain, there are some that will be generic. Your company might have won an award recently, you might have a new director who has huge kudos, you might have acquired a company, etc. – all of these could significantly impact your credibility in the eyes of your prospect and so should be dropped into conversation at the right moment.

High performance tips

- Have a series of anecdotes ready, each of which is associated with a pain that your offering can remove.
- Make sure they're relevant to the prospect and the pain they are experiencing.
- Use anecdotes that show the credibility of your company and its offerings.
- Get a written testimonial corroborating each anecdote.

- Use several anecdotes throughout your Critical Hour to demonstrate your successes in a way that will engage and delight your customers.

19 Discussing value

We have seen how ROI, the value proposition and understanding/ valuing pains all contribute to being able to portray the value of what you offer.

I have also highlighted the difference between a product-pushing sales person and one who listens to and understands the needs and pains of the client and uses that information to think on their feet (one of the elements with greatest impact in the Critical Hour) to create a compelling proposition and reason to buy.

This section allows you to take a bit of a deep dive with the client to get them to agree with the value, rather than cost, of what you are offering.

Therefore it is important that you have worked out the value so you can clearly describe it to the prospect.

One thing to mention here is that too many sales people leave it to the meeting to gather the information they need. So much of that can be garnered over the phone when arranging the meeting. The more information you have prior to this, the better prepared you are – especially for this section of your Critical Hour.

I had a client who took four meetings to close what was a product or transactional sale. At most it should have been two meetings, so their cost of sale was double what it should have been and their sales people were 50 per cent less efficient – they could have been doing more new business pitches per person.

The reason for the four meetings was that they were doing all their fact finding in the first meeting. Some people actually train this approach into sales teams, which is fine when what a company is selling is hugely complex, very involved and takes a lot of investigation and meetings to create the solution. It is not appropriate when someone is selling a fairly straightforward product, service or solution.

You should always know what information you need to uncover in order to know what to pitch, what it will cost and therefore how to discuss its value.

So why can't those questions be asked over the phone in preparation for the meeting? We recommended this to our client and they did reduce the average number of meetings to two. That in turn allowed each sales person to go to more meetings, so not only did their sales cycle decrease but also the volume of sales increased. Simple!

The reason I have emphasised this here is that the more prepared you are for a meeting, the easier it will be for you to really get into a good discussion about the value of what you offer.

High performance tips

- Find out as much information on the phone about the prospect's major pains so you can come to the meeting with a basic value of those pains.
- Reiterate the cost of the pain to the prospect and what you can do to remove it.

- Discuss the value of your offering. In doing this the prospect will not focus so much on the cost.

20 Marketplace understanding

This is where you really need to do your research. Marketplace understanding falls into two categories:

- The marketplace in which **you** operate. Make sure you not only understand your company's products or services but also that you really know your own marketplace. Read all the industry journals and magazines you can get your hands on, do your research on the web of the main players in the industry and your competitors. This will help you to discuss the threats or opportunities that exist in the marketplace and you may be able to highlight some that the prospect was not aware of and how they could relate to them. It also builds the rapport and confidence on both sides.

- The marketplace in which **your prospect** operates. This relates back to the preparation you do for a meeting. Prospects are not keen on sales people that obviously do not understand their marketplace and the competitive pressures within it. So also knowing who their competitors are will really help the confidence of the prospect during the meeting.

> **High performance tip**
>
> Understand both the marketplace in which you operate and the marketplace in which your prospect operates.

21 Differentiation from competition

Being able to differentiate yourself from the competition is probably the most important part of selling if you are trying to protect your margins. If you do not differentiate yourself, you are in a world of 'me too'. In a world of 'me too' the only thing that differentiates is price. Now that may sound OK for many, but just sit and consider the implications of this approach:

- You have no control over your outcomes.
- You give away margin.
- You reduce profitability.
- Price negotiations only go in one direction and that is never upwards.
- You have to attend more meetings to make quota.
- You have to work harder to make quota.
- Every pound you give away in your asking price is a percentage off your pay cheque.

There is a great saying in the world of sales that demonstrates perfectly the problems we face in all industries. It is a stark message, but one that we need to be acutely aware of:

'The world has a surplus of similar companies, employing similar people, with similar educational backgrounds, working in similar jobs, coming up with similar ideas, producing similar things, with similar prices and similar quality.'

In effect, this just tells us that there is a lot of the same out there and it is the job of the sales person to absolutely differentiate their company and offerings from the competition.

Ask any seasoned sales person about how they make themselves different and nearly everyone will tell you that they do this every day. Challenge them to do so, and you get a different outcome. My trainers tell me that in multiple deliveries of the differentiation training programme, it is seen that unique selling points (USPs) and points of differentiation (PODs) are hard to come by. Even for those who have been in the company for years.

Challenge yourself to list 12 different USPs about your company and you may come up with a list that includes some of the points below:

- Great customer service
- Award-winning solution
- Most engineers on the road
- Quickest delivery/installation
- Best in class
- Latest technology
- Newest products on the market

Of course, these are all valid – to a point. The problem with only stating USPs like this, and this is a common situation, is that it leaves the buyer having the opportunity to reply with two, just two, words that will tear your good work apart. What are those two words? *'So what?'*

A very simple question indeed. Countless times it has been seen that not fully forming our USPs can lead to not differentiating at all. We need to demonstrate that we are there to help the customer. We cannot just let them sit there and do the hard work to fill in the gaps to know what our unformed USP means. Not only are we doing ourselves an injustice, but we are also laying ourselves open to the customer misinterpreting the answer.

FORMING A USP

USPs are situational. This means that they match the needs of the buyer in that particular selling situation. This is great news to sales people because, with this information, we have increased our ability to have a much bigger kitbag of USPs.

For example, one of our USPs may be great customer service. Now, that is not to say some of your competition don't also have great customer service, but it may simply come down to who you are up against in any sales situation. Of course this is fundamental information for a sales person to know, so if you are up against company A, and you know their customer service is really poor, then you can state how good yours is and use it as a USP. The situation allows for this. However, if you are also up against company B, who also have great customer service, then you need to find a USP that neutralises both A and B and elevates you above the competition. If you don't, your competition will be leaving you in the 'me too' camp. Good luck with your margins!

Let's look at how a sales situation may go when forming a USP fully.

- **Unformed**

  Sales person: We have the most delivery vans on the road.

  Customer: So what?

- **Formed**

  Sales person: We have the most delivery vans on the road, which means that we are able to solve the problem you are having with failed fulfilment of orders to your customers. Due to the number of vans we have on the road, we can guarantee your deliveries will be completed the next day, thus increasing the efficiency of this part of your operation by 75 per cent.

  Customer: Wow! Now that sounds like something I need to do.

  Sales person: Great. And remember, no other company has the ability to deliver such a service to you.

You get the picture. By fully forming the USP, you are able to outline to the customer what it means to them, its value and the fact that they cannot get this anywhere else. When a solution, product or service is unique and the customer needs it, how easy is it then for them to negotiate on price?

Take a little time to think about and list your top 10 USPs. Make sure that they are fully formed, so that when you pull them out of your kitbag in a sales meeting, the customer is not in a position to say, 'So what?'.

POINTS OF DIFFERENTIATION

Points of differentiation (PODs) are another way in which you can differentiate yourself from the competition. PODs are areas in which you do the same thing, but your product is slightly different in some way. For example, USB memory sticks all hold data, so nothing unique there, but some companies do them in different styles, such as the style of the housing, or the way in which they fold away.

PODs can be broken down into four distinct areas:

- **Product**. Differentiating on the product is a great way in which you can get yourself noticed. There are many ways in which products differentiate themselves. For example, think about vacuum cleaners. For many years, they had a bag to collect the dust and dirt. Then, all of a sudden, we were presented with a bagless vacuum, along with the reasons as to why this is better.

- **Process**. An example here is the way in which we can store and move data around. Until recent times, sending large amounts of electronic data to someone required a physical device, such as a CD, DVD or memory stick. Now we have access to cloud services that make this easier for us. Even within different cloud services there are PODs, with some having delivery features that others do not.

- **People**. This is a somewhat obvious one and easy to say, but we need to be able to articulate exactly how the people make a difference, or it is simply an empty statement. An example of how people can differentiate an organisation is to look at the world of football. In a game of football, it is 11 versus 11. However, the 11 players in a premiership team make a big difference to the success on the field compared to the 11 players that play for a second division side.

- **Partnerships**. Partnerships are an important way in which it is possible to differentiate. What partnerships do you have that make your offering better than the competition? Even the largest companies rely on partnerships to differentiate. For example, certain tablet computer companies rely on other suppliers for componentry. Without the partners to supply such componentry, the overall product may not be so compelling.

It is important to have a good idea of what aspects are available to you to differentiate using PODs. Take a little while to fill in your top five PODs for each of the above areas.

High performance tips

● When describing your point of differentiation, ask yourself, 'So what?' at the end.

● Create different USPs that are based around situations.

● Make sure your USPs are fully formed.

● When forming your PODs, make sure you consider them from a product, process, people and partnership perspective.

---

22 Differentiation from competition when challenged

It is not always appropriate to discuss the competition directly, but sometimes prospects will highlight a competitor's offering and challenge you with their USPs and PODs.

So the point of this section is to say that you *always* need to differentiate your offering whether competitors are mentioned or not, and the prospect should *always* have a good understanding of your USPs and PODs.

However, the prospect may be working with an incumbent or may have just seen a competitor, or you could be in a competitive tender situation. In any of these cases you need to know your competitor's offerings really well and how they price themselves in order to be able to clearly differentiate and help the prospect to understand why it would be better to go with your product or service.

If the prospect has not revealed which competitor they are speaking to, then always ask them who it is. They will not always reveal this to you, which I find really annoying. They won't tell you because they don't want you to go into a direct comparison on that competitor, and it also gives the prospect the feeling of having the upper hand – a sort of smugness. Silly really, as they need to be sure that they are going down the right road and so having a direct comparison can really help their decision. If this is the case then you need to probe the prospect to find out what the competition are offering, what the prospect likes about the competitor and how they compare to what you are offering. Use open questions and the skills from the section above to get the information you need. Then you can differentiate yourself from them.

High performance tip

Always differentiate your offering in every Critical Hour using formed USPs and PODs.

---

23 Product/service knowledge

It may seem blindingly obvious that you need to know your own products and services really well but you'd be surprised how many sales people don't bother to really understand them. From the Cranfield School of Management research referenced earlier, 16 per cent of new business people were narrators and did not know their products well enough to answer questions 'off the script'.

Always remember that there may be some small hidden feature that will really excite the prospect, which you might not have been aware of, or you need to reference when you know what the client's needs or pains are.

It will also be clear to a bright prospect – who may be asking a lot of questions about how your offering would work – that you don't know your own products or services. If that is the case, you have probably just lost the sale.

The description of your products or services needs to include not just the features of each element in your offering but also their benefits. Then fold around that the USPs and PODs and how they match the prospect's pains and needs. This is the place where you can bring many of the elements of the Critical Hour together.

> ## High performance tip
> Make sure you understand your products or services really well, as the smallest feature could make a difference to your Critical Hour.

24 Next steps/timescales

I once went out on a meeting with a senior partner of a top five global accountancy firm to evaluate his capability in a live meeting. He was seeing a relatively small business turning over about £5m with a view to getting them to use their growth service. The meeting was with the two business owners.

The senior partner did all the initial parts of the Critical Hour brilliantly, especially questioning, followed by a compelling description of how the growth service could help them by matching it superbly to their pains. The owners were really pleased and asked, 'This is great, where do we take it from here?'

To my astonishment the partner passed his business card across the table and said, 'Here's my card. Have a think about what I have said and give me a call if you're interested in taking this further.'

I nearly fell off my chair. I could not believe that he had shut them down and got no commitment to any further action or timescales in which to complete those next steps.

NEXT STEPS

As you might imagine, one of the key elements of this section is to ask what the prospect thinks the next steps might be to using your offering. Obviously you need to be clear that they are positive about progressing, otherwise this would be a senseless question.

Next steps could be a myriad of different options, such as:

- Arranging another meeting with a wider audience and key decision makers or people you need to influence.
- Allowing the prospect to go off and work out some numbers that will help you to send a proposal.
- Arranging a time to allow you back to present your proposal.

Whatever the next step is, what you are doing here is progressing the sale, which is vitally important. What you don't want is the prospect to have shown interest and then simply let your Critical Hour end with no further commitment to any action or event.

By getting the prospect to agree to a next step you are confirming their interest in your offering and committing them to an action that will help them towards taking your product or service in the future. What is key here is to make sure you get them to commit to an action that they have to take themselves, otherwise it is just you doing all the running and they are not actually committing to doing anything.

This is also a good way of flushing out any final objections, as most prospects won't commit to a next step that they have to do if they aren't interested.

The best scenario is that you and the prospect have a series of actions and defined responsibilities to progress the deal.

TIMESCALES

Once you have agreed what that next step is going to be, you *must* make sure you get a timescale for completion. The prospect will then know that they have committed to doing something by a certain time; and if they don't, they know you will be chasing them.

Make sure that the timescale is realistic or the prospect will never get to complete it – you'll end up chasing them too early and they will then get annoyed.

Once again, very few prospects like to commit to doing something in a certain timescale unless they are serious about taking your offering. On the flip side, however, you don't want the prospect to set such long timescales that obviously nothing will happen and it makes the sales cycle unrealistic for you: 'Why don't you give me a call back in six months time and we'll see if anything has changed.' This is not a commitment to a next step as they aren't going to do anything and it's all very vague. It's a put off and they aren't interested.

So it is important that you create a sense of urgency. A really good way of doing this is to have identified a compelling event. This is an event or circumstance that is going to occur in the future for which they need to have taken your product or service in order to facilitate it, or much improve the situation when it does happen.

For example, the IT department of a fire and security company could be about to move their whole sales force on to iPads so they can take orders instantly rather than fill in loads of paperwork that could delay the sale, or allow the customer to change their mind and cancel the contract. You might be selling software that processes the order. So the software has to be in place and purchased before they buy the iPads to allow for installation and testing.

The compelling event here is the purchase of the iPads.

DECISION MAKERS

Make sure when agreeing next steps that you discuss participation from the decision makers and confirm or reconfirm who they are. You should have found out during the course of your questioning and listening stage exactly who they are, and if you haven't already, then now is the time to decide how you will approach them to get them on board and committed to taking your offering.

High performance tips

- Agree with the prospect what the next step of the sales cycle is – what is going to happen next as a result of your meeting.
- Get the prospect to commit to a timescale to complete the next step.
- Look for a compelling event in the future that focuses the prospect on setting reasonable timescales.
- If the next step is another meeting then make sure, if you can, that the key decision makers will be present.

---

25 Objection handling

The interesting thing about objection handling is that if you have covered all of the aspects above throughout your Critical Hour then it is unlikely you'll have to handle any objections because you will have allayed any concerns throughout your presentation.

Neil Rackham is the author of *Spin Selling*, which is one of the most commonly used sales techniques in the world today. His book is based on a very solid foundation of research with over 30,000 sales professionals, which he conducted himself. He suggested that transactional sales people could be 'objection creators', by focusing so heavily on their own product's capability that it encourages objection.

Don't think of objections as a bad thing. If your prospect raises an objection then they're discussing their concern, which gives you a chance to answer it. If a prospect is not interested in your product or service then they may offer no objections at all, feign interest and could sit through your presentation in silence. Having their arms crossed can also be a sign that they are resistant to the idea of taking your offering on board.

High Performance tips

● **Listen to the objection**. It is important that you allow the prospect to describe their objection in full. Don't interrupt them because first it is rude, and second you might miss some valuable information from the way in which they phrase their objection or its context. Being interrupted when offering an objection can switch a prospect off altogether.

- **Say it back to the prospect**. Once the prospect is finished stating their objection then repeat what they have said back to them. This will enable you to ensure you have understood it properly and will also allow the prospect to correct you and clarify if not. For example: 'So you're concerned that the project will take up too much time with your managers?' The prospect might qualify: 'Not so much the managers themselves but the project managers in my team.'

- **Ask more exploratory open questions**. The first objection might not be the main one as many prospects will mask the fact that they don't have the money or budget to buy your offering. They may offer objections other than price to avoid the budgetary issue. So it is good to try and get all their objections out on the table. For example: 'What are your project managers working on at the moment that is taking all their time?'

- **Answer the objection**. When you are sure you have understood the objection then go ahead and answer it. Remember that the prospect is offering an objection because they either have not properly understood what you have said or how it would work for them. They may also have a fear about taking your offering so you need to alleviate their anxieties and give them confidence that is OK to do business with you. This is where you can use anecdotes, case studies or market knowledge to show the prospect how similar clients have been really happy with your solution.

- **Make sure the prospect is happy with your answer**. Once you have answered their objection make sure they are happy with what you have said and that it has effectively removed that objection: 'Does that answer your question?'

● **Return to the pitch.** Once you have answered the objection successfully get back to the main thrust of your pitch or pick up from where you left off. Sometimes objections can take you off track, so remind the prospect of what you were discussing by swiftly summarising where you got to before continuing. If you are at the end of your pitch then ensure there are no further objections before moving on to next steps and timescales and closing to the next stage or the deal itself.

26 Creating a solution on the fly

Otherwise known as thinking on your feet – this section of the Critical Hour was rated by Cranfield School of Management as the one that has the biggest impact on the outcome of a successful sale.

It's the magic dust of selling and it is the area that separates the excellent from the average.

This dimension comes with a lot of experience and requires quick thinking. It is where you bring together so many elements of the Critical Hour.

In order to do this you need to have taken on board a good understanding of the client's pains and you must know your marketplace, products and services really thoroughly, as well as the client's marketplace.

It is where you create, or start to create, a solution for the client within the meeting and discuss it with them. A solution is very different to simply offering a product or straightforward service. It is something that is unique to the client and will be something that the client hadn't previously considered.

Creating a solution on the fly can move you quickly to a position of trust with the prospect as you will make them think as opposed to just listening to your pitch. If it is a good solution then the prospect will undoubtedly consider you rather than any competitor.

It also moves any discussion away from one of price to that of value, and so you have instantly become valuable to the prospect.

High performance tips

- Highlight the customer's pain that you identified earlier in the meeting and then discuss your solution, which will remove that pain.
- Create a compelling SVP during the meeting.
- Know your products and services inside out.
- Ensure you have calculated the cost of the pain to the prospect.
- Think from the prospect's side of the table, not yours. What would really help them?

---

27 Closing to the next stage

When we conducted our research with Cranfield School of Management, Professor Lynette Ryals and Professor Neil Rackham agreed that 'closing to the next stage' is one of the most important elements of the sale.

As I point out in the next section on closing, prospects are not always in a position to take your product or services now, or they might need to involve others or go through some internal processes in order to accommodate your offering in their business. So it is important to understand these issues and establish what the next stage of the sales cycle is going to be.

To do this you need to discuss with the prospect what is required to get your product or service into their company. During this discussion you need to constantly reiterate the benefits and ROI of your product or service.

It is also important to point out that there are always different types of 'buyers' in an organisation:

- The person or people who sign the cheque – the **financial buyer**. This is not always the finance or managing director. It could be a manager with a budget or it might be a board of directors.
- The person or people who will use the product or service – the **user buyer**. There will normally be one person or small group who will own this.
- The person who is responsible for installing your product or service into the prospect's company and getting it to work – the **installation buyer**.

- The person who will do the internal selling and convincing of your product or service – the **champion**. They have already bought what you do and are enthused and motivated to get it into their company. Make sure your champion has good kudos and respect within their company. Making a champion of someone who does not command respect is not going to help you – it will make you look as weak as them.

You also need to know the kudos of the different buyers and which one of them will have most weight. You sometimes find that it is not always the financial buyer who will be the most important one (although most times it is). Someone might already have a budget, so it could be more down to how easy the product is to install, for example, so then the installation buyer will be key.

Try to identify who might block the progress of your offering so that you have a plan to either nullify their objection or turn them around to your thinking. So you will need your champion to help you to understand the politics within their company and who the key players are you need to get on board.

These points may all need to be considered, but you obviously don't need to go into this detail if the next stage is a simple one. However, the bigger the value of your offering, then the more of this type of information you need to know.

There may be a number of next stages that need to be agreed and arranged to progress the deal. In some cases you might have to discuss costs with procurement, legal clauses with their lawyer, meet the installation buyer to discuss what it will take to get your offering into the company, and speak to the IT department to get them to plan ahead.

So agree with your prospect what exactly the various next stages are and then set out a plan for each of them with the prospect. Get them to commit and agree to the next stage(s). In some cases you will need to use your closing skills as described in the next section to get agreement to the next stage. However, if your sales value proposition is very strong then you will find that the prospect will be as keen as you are to progress to the next level.

High Performance tips

- Identify what the next stage is.
- Get the prospect to confirm their agreement to that.
- Use closing skills if necessary to get them to commit to the next stage.
- Understand and identify the buyers and key decision makers to be involved in the next stage.

---

28 Closing the deal

I always think that if you have done all your selling properly and have followed the Critical Hour as laid out there is no need to be overtly closing. The conversation should have already moved on to one of 'How are we going to do this?' or 'How are we going to implement it?'

It can also be 'I'm sorry but your offering is not for us' if the prospect is honest, but many people find it hard to say no so will avoid doing so. This is dangerous for you as they can waste your time and create false hope, so it is as important to flush out real interest as much as no interest.

THE TIMING OF SALES

Sales is as much about timing as technique and skill. You may have exactly what they client is looking for but the time is just not now. I have placed this in the closing section of the Critical Hour as I don't want your impatience to get the order to blow out future customers. You can destroy a brilliant future prospect because you tried to close them at the wrong time and did not listen to what they were saying.

Many books will tell you how to create compelling events and close no matter what, but I am not in that camp. The days of hard sales and forcing people to buy things they did not want, or did not need, are long gone as far as I am concerned.

Ethical selling is important if you want to create and maintain a respected brand, have clients come back for more and spread your reputation through good word-of-mouth recommendations.

Remember that bad news travels fast, good news trundles slowly along. You can have a great brand or reputation only for that to come crashing down due to some inappropriate behaviour.

Virtually every time people buy a product or service they will have to change something when they take it on board. Most sales are based around ROI nowadays so you will be providing them with something to help with that.

Think about the purchases you make personally. You normally only buy something when you need it or can afford it. It is the same in business. Companies set annual budgets and have to adhere to them. If they have not budgeted for your offering then they will either need to do so in next year's budget, or make a business case for additional budget in their current financial year.

This all takes time so it is vitally important for you to understand these timescales too.

Sales is also about building a strong pipeline of expected orders, so if a prospect likes what you have to offer, but cannot do anything now for genuine reasons, then accept that and bank it as an order for the future. Time passes quickly and before you know it you will be back to see them in a few months to discuss the progression of the deal, now that they are ready.

The prospect will appreciate this, and if you maintain contact with them over those months it will help you to build a solution with them that will really work. It will also give you a chance to sell to others in their organisation and to build a ground swell of positive opinion towards your company.

CLASSIC CLOSING TECHNIQUES

Some of the techniques of closing are a bit crass and it can often be these high-pressure techniques that get sales people a bad name. They remind me of those two films, *The Boiler Room* and *Glengarry Glen Ross*. If you haven't seen them then go and get hold of a copy now – they are hilarious.

Here is a weblink to some of the funniest clips about sales, which you should also take a look at: **www.peaksalesrecruiting.com/ greatest-sales-movies-of-all-time**

This is a list of the different ways in which you could conduct a close (taken from **www.changingminds.org**)

- 1-2-3 close – close with the principle of three.
- Adjournment close – give them time to think.
- Affordable close – ensure people can afford what you are selling.
- Alternative close – offer a limited set of choices.
- Artisan close – show the skill of the designer.
- Ask-the-manager close – use the manager as authority.
- Assumptive close – act as if they are ready to decide.
- Balance-sheet close– add up the pros and the cons.
- Best-time close – emphasise how now is the best time to buy.
- Bonus close – offer delighter to clinch the deal.
- Bracket close – make three offers, with the target in the middle.
- Calculator close – use calculator to do discount.
- Calendar close – put it in the diary.
- Companion close – sell to the person with them.
- Compliment close – flatter them into submission.
- Concession close – give them a concession in exchange for the close.
- Conditional close – link closure to resolving objections.
- Cost of ownership close – compare cost over time with competitors.
- Courtship close – woo them to the close.
- Customer-care close – the customer care manager calls you later and reopens the conversation.
- Daily cost close – reduce cost to daily amount.
- Demonstration close – show them the goods.
- Diagram close – draw a picture that pulls them in.

- Distraction close – catch them in a weak moment.
- Doubt close – show you doubt the product and let them disagree.
- Economic close – help them pay less for what they get.
- Embarrassment close – make *not* buying embarrassing.
- Emotion close – trigger identified emotions.
- Empathy close – empathise with them, then sell to your new friend.
- Empty-offer close – make them an empty offer that the sale fills.
- Exclusivity close – reveal that not everyone can buy this.
- Extra Information close – give them more information to tip them into closure.
- Fire Sale close – offer soiled goods, going cheap.
- Future close – close on a future date.
- Give-take close – give something, then take it away.
- Golden bridge close – make the only option attractive.
- Handover close – hand over to someone else to do the final close.
- Handshake close – offer handshake to trigger automatic reciprocation.
- Humour close – relax them with humour.
- Hurry close – go fast to stop them thinking too much.
- IQ close – say how this is for intelligent people.
- Minor points close – close first on the small things.
- Never-the-best-time close – use for customers who are delaying.
- No-hassle close – make it as easy as possible.
- Now-or-never close – to hurry things up.

- Opportunity cost close – show the cost of not buying.
- Ownership close – act as if they own what you are selling.
- Price-promise close – promise to meet any other price.
- Puppy close – act cute to invoke sympathy and a nurturing response.
- Quality close – sell on quality, not on price.
- Rational close – use logic and reason.
- Repetition close – repeat a closing action several times.
- Requirements close – write down what they want as a formal requirement.
- Retrial close – go back to square one.
- Reversal close – act as if you do not want them to buy the product.
- Save-the-world close – buy now and help save the world.
- Selective-deafness close – respond only to what you want to hear.
- Shame close – make not buying shameful.
- Shopping list close – tick off a list of their needs.
- Similarity close – bond them to a person in a story.
- Standing-room-only close – show how others are queuing up to buy.
- Summary close – tell them all the things they are going to receive.
- Testimonial close – use a happy customer to convince the new customer.
- Thermometer close – they score out of ten, you close gap.
- Think about it close – give them time to think about it.
- Treat close – persuade them to 'give themselves a treat'.
- Trial close – see if they are ready for a close.

- Valuable customer close – offer them a special 'valued customer' deal.
- Ultimatum close – show negative consequences of not buying.
- Yes-set close – get them saying 'yes' and they'll keep saying 'yes'.

ASK FOR THE ORDER

If you are in a situation where the prospect is still procrastinating and you can see that they are still not sure whether to go ahead or not, then here are some tips.

Never be afraid to ask them for the order. This might seem a basic requirement but so many sales people have either assumed the prospect will go ahead but didn't ask, or were too shy to ask for the order.

Some of the closing techniques above are a good way of asking for the order, as they can be turned into well-constructed questions:

'So when would you like to start the project?

'Would you like to take the order before the end of the quarter?'

And there are many more examples.

If you have asked for the order or you are proposing a price for your services, be silent thereafter. A nervous or unconfident sales person will carry on talking, often trying to justify what they have just said or asked for.

Don't do this! You need to see what the prospect is going to say and then react. By being silent you will make the prospect feel uncomfortable and will force them to respond. That tension is deliberate as it forces change – they need to move from where they have been to a new place and you're helping them do that. It is OK to do this.

Asking for the order will usually invoke one of four reactions:

1   They will discuss and agree and you'll move to a conclusion.
2   They will not agree and will voice an objection.
3   They will want to think about it or speak to others in their organisation.
4   They will ask for a proposal.

With option 1 you are on your way to closing a deal but you may need to negotiate (see below).

With option 2 you can use the methodology laid out in objection handling above.

With option 3 they have moved to the famous 'pause' button. Always explore the 'speak to others' option. Who do they need to speak to and why? What are they hoping to achieve by speaking to them and when will they do that? (But don't ask these questions as directly as written.) Check if you can speak to them too, remembering that the prospect in front of you will never be able to sell your offering as well as you. It is quite often worth reminding the prospect of that.

If they are happy for you to be involved then you know you are progressing the deal well. Discuss what they'd like you to do when presenting to their colleagues. You need to establish if the prospect is genuine or just saying that to get you out.

Quite often a wider group or next meeting stage will involve a key decision maker, so it is important to discuss the meeting and what the people in the room will be looking for with the prospect. This is where you can start to build the 'champion' in your prospect – the person who will sell your proposition internally and be highly supportive of it. If they are serious about preparing for this meeting they will arrange a time to do so.

REQUEST FOR A PROPOSAL

Option 4 will often be used by a prospect to get rid of you. Don't always see this as a positive. If they have asked for a proposal all too quickly and with not enough conviction then you need to probe them for what they want and by when.

If they have done this as a result of a fair bit or extensive discussion around how it would work, when it would start etc. then it is likely that it is a genuine request. Always ask when they would like the proposal by and confirm that you would like to come back and present it to them or, if that is not convenient, the very least you would expect is a phone call to go through it.

Too many sales people make the mistake of just emailing the proposal and expecting the prospect to drop everything and read it. Remember they are busy people and you're unlikely to be the biggest priority for them at this time.

So find time in their diary to give your proposal the attention and discussion it needs, which will also enable you to get your offering further up their priority list.

By discussing your proposal with them rather than simply sending it, you set up a further closing stage to give you the opportunity to discuss any further objections or concerns, and timescales for implementation or delivery. You can then repeat this stage once more.

ONE-NIGHT STAND?

In most business relationships companies are trying to build a long-term relationship over time with their clients. They would either like repeat or incremental business from them, or for them to recommend their brand through word of mouth as they have had such a great experience.

So many companies will need coaxing, convincing and wanting to feel courted so they are sure you understand them and their business before they give you the order.

This is similar to most personal relationships that last for a period of time. They take time and effort to build and maintain. One-night stands don't. It's all about closing the deal and wham, bang, thank you ma'am. Many are not brilliant experiences, which one might regret and wouldn't want repeated. So ask yourself – are you going for one-night stands or lasting relationships? Then think about how aggressively you want to close.

High performance tips

● Don't sell someone something they don't need – ethical selling should be your mantra, otherwise a sale will come back and bite you.

● Find out the timescales for a sale. If it is not now, it may well be in the future.

● Don't discard a prospect that did not buy this time round. They were interested so may well buy in a year or two – stay in contact.

● Learn the different types of closes so you can pick the most appropriate at the time.

● Ask for the order.

● Once you ask for the order or have delivered your side of the negotiation, keep quiet. Silence is your friend!

● Make sure a request for a proposal is genuine. You don't want to waste your time with people who can't say no.

● Don't be impatient, but look to build long-term relationships.

29 Negotiation throughout the meeting

Those of us that began our sales career in the trenches, on the front line, have probably been told by our peers and/or overenthusiastic line managers that negotiation begins from the very first moment that you make contact with a prospective client.

This includes constant negotiation with gatekeepers to be put through to relevant people, negotiation with influencers to get additional contact details of decision makers, and ensuring relevant people are championing our solution in preference to one of our competitors, not forgetting the actual negotiation with decision makers regarding dates and costings, etc.

Although I believe that what I was told is partly true, I have come to learn that there is a lot more to influencing people than just what is said to be 'negotiation'.

Influencing others involves not only negotiation but also persuasion. Persuasion is the ability to convince others to take action on a particular point that they may not have thought about or wanted to act on without your influence.

Persuasion, is used to influence people throughout the entire sales process. In contrast, negotiation is used far less often and usually towards the end of the sales process or Critical Hour – to discuss and reach a mutually agreed conclusion or agreement.

LAWS OF PERSUASION

According to Robert Cialdini (in his book *Influence: The Psychology of Persuasion*) there are six laws of persuasion:

1 Reciprocity
2 Commitment and consistency
3 Social proof
4 Authority
5 Liking
6 Scarcity

Over the years I have found that these laws form the basis of almost all situations in which someone is attempting to influence another to take action on a particular point that they may not have thought of previously. Let's take some time to explain each law and think about how they are evident in everyday situations.

Reciprocity

When you give something to someone, they feel compelled to return the favour. They feel bad if they don't reciprocate. Similarly, this includes instances when someone turns down a large request. Assuming the request is positioned correctly, they are then more likely to agree to a smaller one. Think how you could include elements of this law into your selling approach.

Commitment and consistency

Consistency is seen as a desirable human attribute and it is associated with strength, honesty and stability. People will do more to remain consistent with their commitments if they have already taken a small initial step. Therefore, if you can get someone to do you a small favour, they are more likely to grant you a larger one later on. Furthermore, thanking them for their efforts and informing them of its benefits will greatly increase the chances of larger favours in future. Think of a time when you have seen this law in action.

Social proof

We view a behaviour as more likely to be correct the more we see others performing it. We assume that if a lot of people are doing the same thing, they must know something that we don't. This behaviour is strongest when we are uncertain; therefore we are more likely to trust in the collective knowledge of the crowd. What can you do to make the most of this innate behaviour?

Authority

We are more likely to comply with someone who is (or resembles) an authority. In other words, people prefer to take advice from 'experts'. There is a deep-seated duty to authority within us learned from parents, school, religious authorities, etc. Think how you convey your expertise to your prospects and clients.

Liking

We are more inclined to follow the lead of someone who is similar to us rather than someone who is dissimilar. We learn better from and are more likely to help people who are similar to us. We even prefer people whose names are similar to ours. Similarly, it is very important to remember and use people's names. For example, others are more likely to like you and respond to you if you say 'Hello, Sarah' rather than just 'Hello'. Think how you can highlight similarities in a tactful and subtle way.

Scarcity

Items are more valuable to us when their availability is limited. Scarcity can determine the value of an item. For example, if a customer is told that an item is in short supply or is available at that price for only a limited time, then they are more likely to buy it. Furthermore, if something is expensive, we tend to assume that it must be of higher quality because it is in demand. How do others perceive the value of your offering in accordance with this law?

Being aware of these six laws will enhance your position when influencing others, as well as when being influenced by others. Also, consciously using them on a regular basis throughout your own Critical Hour will increase the number of opportunities you have that reach the real negotiation stage.

AGREEING TERMS

Negotiation should only begin once both parties have agreed that they are interested in working with each other and it is just down to agreeing the terms of the deal in order to seal it.

When negotiating complex deals you often find there will be a number of items that need negotiating. For example, in my business we sell large training contracts associated with the use of proprietary competency frameworks and technology that we license, so there are a number of elements that need to be agreed:

- The overall amount of work to be delivered
- The timeline in which it needs to be delivered
- The ownership of the intellectual property
- The cost of the training per day
- The licence fee
- The service level agreement

There will always be areas that you are prepared to give on and ones that you won't be willing to concede. So make sure that you get the prospect's stance on all contentious elements before starting with negotiation from your end.

If you don't contemplate problem areas, you can spend a lot of time discussing just one part of the overall deal, which could get quite heated and difficult. What you don't want to end up with is an impasse where neither side will back down. If you know there are other areas that you could concede on, then that will make the negotiator feel like they have been given something and they will more than likely become more flexible on other points.

There is a lot of ego in negotiation. You see poor negotiators resort to bullying and threats in order to get their way. I remember one sales director I dealt with over a number of years was like this. He would say, 'Well, I think we need to pull the whole deal and look to your competitors' or 'Unless you give me this price I will stop the whole programme and we will kick out your whole methodology.'

It is hard to negotiate with these types of people as they are effectively resorting to blackmail and that is the lowest form of negotiation.

At one point that director did go with an alternative solution with a competitor for a sales manager assessment solution, only to find that a year later the whole exercise had been a total waste of time. He was none the wiser about the capability of his managers and he had wasted thousands of pounds.

BEHAVIOUR STYLES

There is one psychological profiling model regularly referred to in negotiation, which uses profiles developed by David Merrill and Roger Reid (who drew on earlier work by Fred Fiedler).

It is a simple questionnaire that you can take and score within 20 minutes. It will provide you with your primary and secondary behaviour style; there are four styles used to create any primary and secondary combination, as follows:

1 Expressive

2 Supportive

3 Driver

4 Analytic

Knowing your own behaviour style is very useful. Even more beneficial is to be able to accurately predict the behaviour style of the person with whom you are about to enter negotiations. This is because different behaviour styles prefer to negotiate and be sold to in different ways.

Expressive

Expressive buyers are personable, social and often have a sense of humour. They are flexible, creative and open to change. They are big-picture thinkers and often have little need for details. To build rapport with expressive buyers, take the time to begin the negotiation on a social note. Be creative in your solutions and focus on coming up with a number of viable options. When you reach agreement on details, make sure that the deal points are clarified and specific before finalising the negotiation.

Supportive

These people are easy buyers to get an appointment with but the most difficult buyers to complete the sale with.

Buyers who use the supportive behaviour style have a strong need to feel recognised and valued in the negotiating partnership. They have a strong concern for relationships, so they tend to focus more on feelings and less on facts.

They will often begin a negotiation with social conversation that is unrelated to the negotiation. They are trusting, optimistic and generally committed to outcomes that benefit both parties.

To build rapport with your supportive buyer, be sincere, show genuine respect and care. Remain positive and solution-oriented. Do not go head to head in a confrontational manner, which will most likely cause them to retreat and end the negotiation.

Driver

Drivers have a strong concern for outcomes and, when ruthlessly pursuing their goal, may become shark-like. They tend to be impatient, have little need for detailed information, and want to move the negotiation to closure quickly. Drivers are self-confident, assertive and, when feeling cornered, may become aggressive in their tactics. Winning is all-important.

Preparation is critical when negotiating with a driver. Know your bottom line. Be prepared and keep your interactions focused on business. This will help you remain assertive, direct, focused and succinct. Understand that when negotiating with a driver, however ruthless your counterpart becomes, it's not personal, just business from the driver's perspective.

Analytical

True analytical buyers methodically explore all options, leaving no stone unturned in their quest for a fair and economical outcome.

Analytical buyers have a strong need for facts and details, and won't move forward unless they have had the opportunity to carefully analyse all available data.

To build rapport and gain respect from your analytical buyer, do your homework before the negotiation begins. Make sure your research is complete and accurate. Keep your discussions factual and business-related. Be honest and ethical, and demonstrate ways in which outcomes will be advantageous in terms of money, time or resources conserved.

When you present information regarding your product or service to an analytical buyer, always present both the pros and cons. Finally, be patient and respect their need to process information methodically and in their own time.

Obviously it is not possible to ask your prospect or client to complete a behaviour style questionnaire before you need to engage in any negotiation with them, although it is possible to determine which of the behaviour styles they do fit into and adjust your approach accordingly. It plays an important part in any skilled negotiator's preparation.

PLANNING AND PREPARATION

Planning and preparation is actually an integral part to any negotiation for both the buyer and the seller.

A training manager of a company that sold top-of-the-range trucks, which were the most expensive on the market, once asked me to drop my price by 35 per cent from £120,000 to £80,000 because that was what my competitor was offering.

I explained that there was no comparison between what we were going to deliver in terms of quality and quantity. It was a bit like buying a cheap van compared to a state-of-the-art truck.

The second thing I pointed out was that the manager wanted us to find out why his sales guys were not able to sell the value of their trucks by assessing their sales capability and then fixing the problem with some training. Getting their clients to understand the value of what they were offering so they maintained their profit margin was crucial.

And yet he was asking me to cut 35 per cent off my price even though, when I went through the difference in what we were proposing to do compared to the competition, he understood we were offering much more all round.

I also pointed out that if I were to deliver the work at that price then we would make no profit. Something in which he appeared totally disinterested. So I walked away from the deal.

You have to go into every negotiation knowing what your 'walk away' point is. One valuable negotiation tool that helps with preparing and planning for negotiation is known as LIMWAP, an acronym we use when teaching sales people this simple negotiation process.

It stands for:

- Like
- Intend
- Must
- Walk-away point

LIMWAP is mostly related to preparation and planning, because it encourages the sales person to decide what each of these stages looks like and therefore allows us to enter into negotiations with an offer that we would **like** to get, dropping back to what we **intend** to get and if necessary settling on what we **must** get.

There is also a final stage that we must be aware of, and that is our **walk-away point**, as demonstrated in the story above.

SKILLED NEGOTIATION

The profile of a skilled negotiator is made of four key elements: two have been partly explored already in this chapter – **process** and **relationship**.

- **Process** includes correct preparation and planning, as well as appropriate techniques that help with objection handling and closing whilst negotiating.
- **Relationship** not only includes relationship-building versatility, meaning how well can you adapt your behaviour style to suit others, but also your negotiation-response preference: how you prefer to respond to negotiation.

The other two elements are less complex, although they are equally important – **value** and **vision**.

- **Value** refers to perceived value, not value for money. One way to increase perceived value is to use tradeables and return concessions in every negotiation. What have you got that doesn't cost much, although is perceived as high value to the prospect or client, e.g. higher level of service, additional licence length, or preferable payment terms? Similarly, what has the prospect or client got that doesn't cost much and is of high value to you, e.g. an earlier decision date, referrals, or promise of a written testimonial?

- **Vision** requires good communication skills to identify and establish the accurate needs of both parties and therefore the creation of a 'shared vision'. It is often referred to as win-win negotiating, as opposed to win-lose or lose-win. The latter two are actually temporary because eventually they will revert to lose-lose. This occurs either when the client becomes extremely dissatisfied because what they had initially agreed to does not meet their expectations, or when the sales person begins to resent the client because the pain is not congruent with the pleasure that the account had initially brought.

Reflect on these four elements following any sales opportunity and you will find that you will have a natural preference to focus on one or two and therefore may neglect the others.

Remember that a truly skilled negotiator will be able to utilise all four elements as necessary and with maximum impact in all sales opportunities.

High performance tips

- Make sure you understand the difference between negotiation and persuasion.
- Learn the six laws of persuasion:
  1 Reciprocity – giving something compels a return favour.
  2 Commitment and consistency – stay consistent with your commitments.

3   Social proof – people think a behaviour is correct the more people they see doing it.

4   Authority – we comply with someone who is (or resembles) an authority.

5   Liking – we tend to follow the lead of someone who is similar to us rather than someone who is dissimilar.

6   Scarcity – items are more valuable to us when their availability is limited.

● Negotiation should only begin once both parties have agreed that they are interested in working with each other.

● Understand all the elements that can be open to negotiation.

● Always have a clear goal for how you want the negotiation to end.

● Know your behaviour style and that of your prospect:

1   Expressive – personable, social types who are big-picture thinkers and often have little need for details.

2   Supportive – these types have a strong need to feel recognised and valued in the negotiating partnership.

3   Driver – these people are impatient, have little need for detailed information, and want to move the negotiation to closure quickly.

4   Analytical – these types have a strong need for facts and details, and won't move forward unless they have had the opportunity to carefully analyse all available data.

- Understand what you would **like** to get, dropping back to what you **intend to get** and if necessary settle on what you **must** get.
- Make sure you are clear on your **walk-away point** before you enter into a negotiation.
- Make sure you end your negotiation in a win-win situation where both parties are happy.

Measurement of the basic sales cycle

This chapter has been added for managers who are not sure what a basic sales cycle or sales process is or how to measure it.

Opportunity checklist

When analysing a deal in your pipeline you should be asking the following opportunity questions:

- What is the customer's budget?
- When can they spend that budget?
- What are their preferred timescales for implementing the solution?
- Who is involved in the decision making?
- What is their pain?
- What positive impact will your solution have?
- Have you quantified that impact on the client?
- Have you told the client about that impact?
- Are you talking to the right people?
- How do you know who all the right people are?
- Why do they want to buy from your team rather than the competition?
- Who else are they talking to?
- What if they do nothing?
- What type of questions are you asking?

There are many more questions one could ask but I can guarantee that most sales people will not be able to answer those above about all their opportunities. And this is basic stuff.

Measuring the sales pipeline

There are different stages to a making a new business sale, which constitute the sales process that you should follow. The stages can also be used to measure the progress of your sales pipeline. These stages will differ according to the sophistication of what you are selling (short term versus long term, length of time to make the sale) and can include:

1 Creating a set of leads
2 Making an appointment
3 First presentation
4 Creation of a proposal
5 Second presentation to present the proposal
6 Negotiation
7 Legal contract
8 Close

If you allocate a probability percentage next to each stage then you will be able to start forecasting revenues from your pipeline. For example, you might allocate the following probability percentages to these stages:

1	Creating a set of leads	0%
2	Making an appointment	0%
3	First presentation	10%
4	Creation of a proposal	40%
5	Second presentation to present the proposal	50%
6	Negotiation	70%
7	Legal contract	90%
8	Close	100%

So if you have £100,000 of revenue at stage 4 at 40 per cent, £150,000 at stage 5 at 50 per cent and £50,000 at stage 6 at 70 per cent, then your total pipeline revenue equals £150,000.

Mindset and application

So how are you feeling about new business selling now? You now have a path to follow for best practice in your Critical Hour. If you're a manager of sales people, you have a methodology to embed and coach into the team, which will really drive the success of your new business meetings, and ultimately your revenues.

There is, however, another really important factor in new business selling without which you will not be successful – your mindset and motivation.

As mentioned at the start of the book, the core DNA of a sales person is tenacity, resilience and curiosity. Why is that? Well, unsurprisingly, when you go out into the world to sell your products or services, not everyone will want to buy them and competition will be between strong and fierce.

People will tell you to give up, that everyone else is doing it, or prospects will not be ready for what you have to offer, or perhaps it simply isn't for them. So your ability to ignore the negative thoughts and feelings (often created by others) is going to be the difference between your success or failure.

Let's just look at what those words mean, according to the Oxford English Dictionary.

TENACITY

> 'The quality of being determined to do or achieve something. Firmness of purpose, doggedness, perseverance, persistence, persistency.'

Notice the use of the word 'quality' in the definition above. Yes, tenacity is a quality, which many people don't appreciate.

My definition is 'Never give up', which is probably something I will have written as my epitaph.

The one thing you can be sure of in sales is that it is a tough job. You're as good as your last month, quarter or year. You could end a year and be a superstar, only to start a new year the same as everyone else and having to begin again. I believe that the selling only really starts when you get a 'No'. If you truly feel that the prospect will be better off with your offering in their company then don't be put off when the initial response is 'No, thanks'. I can't tell you how many of my deals started there but, after persevering over time, the prospects realised they needed what I was selling.

Sometimes it's just down to timing, so you need to keep the selling going for a year or two, but never take people off your list unless you think that what you're offering has no value to them.

Tenacity will also apply to how you go about prospecting. You need to call, contact and speak to a lot of people to create a good pipeline of meetings and companies who are interested in your offering. So don't give up on prospecting – keep going – because sales is also a numbers game. However, don't take a scattergun approach to your prospecting – target specific sectors and types of companies that match the optimum profile for ideal customer.

RESILIENCE

'The capacity to recover quickly from difficulties; toughness.'

This is essential for sales people. If you cannot handle disappointment then do not entertain the thought of a job in sales. Sales is about taking someone from a place where they had no idea about your product or service, or no initial interest, to them wanting to buy it.

Getting someone to buy something they want is taking an order – that is simple, and it is not selling.

The huge psychological step in going from a no to a yes and parting with your money in the process is massive. Being able to persuade someone to do that is a real skill.

There have been countless meetings I have attended with sales people over the years where, as we have left, they have thought they had the sale in the bag. In fact all they did was make a good product demonstration and because the customers showed interest and thought it was quite sound, they had assumed they would buy it. However they couldn't have been further from the truth.

In the UK we suffer from being polite and would rather not say what we think in order to avoid confrontation. So when a sales person asks the prospect if they would like a proposal, they will say yes. So many sales people assume this is as good as a done deal.

So the sales person spends lots of time writing a proposal, sends it off and then calls and calls to try to discuss it. The deal goes into the pipeline and keeps drifting through the pipeline as time goes on. The reality is that the prospect was never interested in the first place.

How to avoid disappointment
Here are a few tips on how to handle or avoid that disappointment.

- First make sure you have plenty of other realistic opportunities in the pipeline. That way if you lose one then you won't be totally dependent on it.

- Make sure that you ask the customer the right questions so you know that you can definitely expect the order:
  - When would you like to take the product or service?
  - Is there any more information you need from me in order to make a decision?
  - Who is involved in the decision-making process? Do I need to meet any of them?
  - Do you have what you need to internally present the case to take on my product/service?
  - Do you have the budget approved to buy my offering?
  - Are you considering any other options?
  - Do you have any reservations?

These questions will enable you to handle your expectations and thus the timing and stage of your pipeline so surprises are kept to a minimum.

- Do not assume anything. Base your predictions and expectations on facts, not fiction, or what you want to hear.

- Be realistic in your expectations. It is better to downplay the size of a deal than over-egg it, otherwise you will disappoint yourself and those around you.

- Make sure you are clear with the prospect about exactly who and how many people are making decisions. There are always more than one, so you need to find them. It is not always the person signing the cheque. There are people who will use the product or service, people who might have to install it or make changes to take your offering into the company. They can all discuss the merits of your offering and influence the final decision.

- Make sure you get to meet all the people involved and handle any concerns they might have directly. No prospect will sell your product better than you.

CURIOSITY

'A strong desire to know or learn something.'

Curiosity relates to questioning and listening. People who have curiosity like to understand the 'why' and like to dig to find out. Their natural tendency is to probe and discover facts and causes, which is essential for selling.

This is a key skill in our modern world of sales. As I have described at some length, sales is all about understanding your potential customers' needs and pains. It's about building solutions that they really want to buy and which will genuinely add value to their business. Therefore those people that have a tendency to want to learn and find out more about the people they interact with will be better suited to the current era of sales. Those that just want to push their products and pressurise people into committing to things they won't see any value in are stuck in the old way of selling – otherwise known as bullies.

Realising and accepting change

Before I discuss what you should be doing to get your whole persona and mental state into the most positive it can be, I need to talk about change.

One of the biggest challenges with trying to change someone's sales capability is getting them to accept they need to change in the first place. The very attributes you want in a sales person – confidence and self-belief – can work against the learning process.

The change curve described below is a brilliant illustration of what people go through when faced with change, no matter how big or small the situation. Change is one thing that will be constant in your life. It's like the wind, you cannot stop it and it will always exist. So if you're a person who likes calm and things to be consistently the same, then go and live on a desert island, because anywhere else there will be continual change.

A man I admire and have spent a lot of time with is Brian Mayne, who created Goal Mapping. He has one of the most moving personal stories I have heard and is an excellent example of someone who, through their own immense volition and against all odds, became successful and has now helped millions of others improve their lives. Brian speaks of change and compares it to the wind. He is a keen sailor and makes a superb analogy. You can either be blown by the wind and be out of control, having no idea where you're going or where you'll end up, and often crash into rocks and have to start again, or you can harness the wind and tack into it, setting your own clear course of where you want to get to and allowing the wind to help you get there.

That vision resonated with me in a big way as in sales there is also constant change. You have to be prepared for deals that you thought you were going to win to move or drop out due to internal change within your prospect organisation. You also need to accept that your circumstances will change and that you also need to continue to develop your skills. If you take a positive stance on this and accept change when it is needed or happens, then you'll get on in life a lot faster.

Setting goals helps reduce the unpredictability of your life and enables you to clearly aim for things you want to achieve. It is just the same with sales, where you have targets to achieve so you know what you need to do.

When I was younger I toured Australia and in one of my lonelier moments I met someone who suggested that if I write down all the attributes of my perfect woman in a lot of detail and kept that paper on my person, I would meet them within months.

I had about 12 dates, then on 13 October 2005 I met my wife and soulmate on a date in a bar in Smithfields, which we had arranged online. She was exactly as I had imagined my perfect woman to be a year previously. So much so that I read out the description at our wedding in Greve in Italy in 2008 – amazing everyone that knew her by how accurate it was.

This story is not only a good tip if you're single and looking for love, but also highlights that life is full of change and it will never be stable. It is how you go about harnessing that change that will define your success.

High performance tips

- Accept that change is constant, so you always need to adapt.
- Set goals to focus your direction through both good and turbulent times.
- Keep positive mentally at all times.

The change curve

To explain the change curve (Figure 6.1) let me use the example of driving.

The very first time you sit in the driving seat of a car you think that it will be easy. You don't know what you don't know, so why would you think anything else? You are **unconsciously incompetent** or, in other words, you have no idea how bad you are.

My 17-year-old son did just that – sat in my car thinking it would be easy and got out 20 minutes later saying it was one of the hardest things he'd tried to do. Naturally he stalled the car and was totally confused by the different functions of the pedals and gears. At this stage he hadn't even got on the road!

Figure 6.1 The change curve

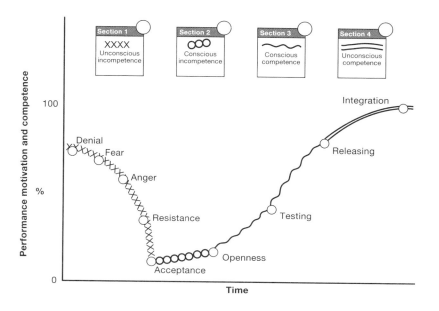

Very quickly my son moved to **conscious incompetence** – he realised how poor he was and how much he had to learn before he would be able to drive. More importantly he moved to accepting he had to change his approach and that it would take time and a lot of practice to do so. This is the most important step on the change curve.

Then as he practised and had lessons, the learner driver started to understand what he had to do to be able to drive proficiently. He then puts those skills and lessons into practice, but had to think hard about what he was doing and when to do it. He was **consciously competent** or, in other words, thinking hard and concentrating on what he needed to do.

Now, if you have been driving for a while, think about the last time you drove a car. Did you think consciously about changing gear, braking, looking in the mirror, etc.? Probably not, because you are **unconsciously competent**. Those skills are so ingrained within you that you don't even think about them – they are 'business as usual' skills.

If you follow the Critical Hour approach and you get into a position where you're not even consciously thinking about using the new skills described, then you will be a master sales person and your revenues and deal closing will be very high.

When it comes to developing yourself or training sales people, the first thing you have to do is get to a place where you or they *accept the need to change*, otherwise you or they won't.

How many training courses have you been on where you have spent the morning deciding whether you like, trust and believe the trainer? Once you do, you are open to learning and may even take something on board.

How many training courses have you been on where you didn't want to go? Where you sat through the course thinking it was a waste of time? Where you were not going to learn because you were not interested? Where you did not accept you needed the training, you were only there because you were told to go?

How many courses were a waste of time because you were already versed in the material and skills? Many companies send people on courses as a way of 'inoculation'. 'Everyone's been through the course therefore they now know the material and are using it in everyday business.' What a load of rubbish. The naivety of organisations staggers me all the time.

The point is that when people accept they need the training their openness to learning and retention of the information goes through the roof.

ASSESSING STRENGTHS AND WEAKNESSES

I developed a way of getting sales people to the point of acceptance at astonishing speed by assessing them objectively against best practice role profiles that are relevant to the sales job they do in their company and presenting the results as a report for that person. One of those is the Critical Hour for new business sales people.

In the Critical Hour report you can see the strengths and weaknesses of an individual or team. By taking the sales person through this report, it quickly moves them to a point of acceptance. That's the beauty of sales people. When they see the point and what's in it for them, they get on with it immediately.

We also use this data to create tailored training programmes. What one team may get in terms of a training course will be different to another, based on their reports.

That means when the sales person enters the training workshop they are at the point of acceptance from 9am, not 12 noon! They learn and remember more to apply thereafter.

This method ticks a number of boxes:

- It gets the sales person to accept they need to change.
- It shows them where they need to change and do so sustainably.
- It makes sure they receive relevant skills training by removing material irrelevant to them and ensuring they concentrate on pertinent issues.
- additionally it provides a coaching platform for the sales manager to use after the course to ensure sustainability, and means that the sales person uses these new skills as part of business as usual.

High performance tips

- You have to accept change before you embrace it. No one will change anything they do until they have accepted change is necessary.
- Whilst getting to the point where you accept change, your performance will drop. Once you are getting on with change, your performance will increase.

The power of your mind

I have learnt a number of things that I now know as fact, truth and reality, which many people still struggle to comprehend.

I often ask audiences what they consider to be the most powerful thing in the world and I always get mixed responses, such as the President of the USA, a nuclear bomb, money, viruses and many more examples. However, no one yet has given me what I believe is the correct answer.

The most powerful thing in the world is **your mind**. It is what will make or break your world. The only thing that you really have in this world is you. Without you, you have nothing, as you will not exist. You can therefore master and make your destiny or you can drift through life letting things happen to you.

Henry Ford once said, 'If you think you can, you can. If you think you can't, you can't, and either way you'll prove yourself right.'

The fact of the matter is that things do not happen to you. You make them happen. The sooner you realise that – in life, business and especially sales – the quicker you will deal with change, harness the wind and get to where you want to be.

You pull things in towards yourself by the way you think and how you act as a result of those thoughts. You can do anything you want to. The bigger and more challenging the thing, the more effort and dedication you will have to put into it to achieve it. Having the first thought to do it is the first step to achieving your goal. You now have possibilities, you will still have to work hard to achieve the goal, but at least now you know where you're going.

How many times have you been thinking or talking about someone and they phone you? Coincidence? No. There is no such thing as coincidence.

Brian Mayne wrote a book called *Sam the Magic Genie,* which is a story for kids about positive thinking and its benefits. I have given away over 200 copies to adults so far, because it is such a powerful story.

I read it to my children when they were 9 and 7. Ryan, my 9-year-old son at the time, was very much an 'I can't do that' boy. The story and my constant reference to the story changed him to an 'I can' boy.

Ryan wanted to be a rugby player. He set out to be as fit as possible at a young age. He won player of the season most seasons at Tunbridge Wells Rugby Club and now he plays for Sevenoaks (Kent), Saracens U18 Academy and has played for England at U16 – the highest level of rugby you can play at his age. He focused on that goal at 10 and worked hard to achieve it.

My daughter Jaydee has been one of the most positive and happy people I have met in my life, and she still refers to the book at the age of 15.

High performance tips
- The most powerful thing in the world is your mind.
- You make things happen: things don't happen to you.
- The thoughts you think can happen, so be careful what you wish for.

The conscious and subconscious mind

Brian Mayne told me about the conscious and subconscious mind. The conscious mind can only see words and is the leadership/ logical side of your brain. The subconscious mind can only see pictures and is the creative side. What I didn't realise is that the subconscious cannot make decisions or value judgements. It cannot see good or evil, can't say yes or no. It simply does what it is told by the conscious mind, which acts as the captain of the ship – giving orders. And yet 80 per cent of what we do every day is down to the subconscious mind.

Have you ever driven somewhere and cannot remember the journey? That's because your conscious mind has decided the destination and the subconscious mind has got you there, while the conscious mind thought about other things during that time.

How often do you tell yourself that you feel bad today, that this meeting isn't going to go well, that the company is not going to give you the order, that you're not going to hit target, that he doesn't like you, etc.?

Whatever you think, you're directing your subconscious towards that event or circumstance. Think positive and suddenly you'll find you're a lot more successful and happier. Simple, eh?

Well, yes it is. If you're thinking that what you've just read is a load of baloney, then it will pass you by. To you things will come about because you've just told your subconscious that it is, so it will be.

To me it works and my life is real evidence that it does. Ask my wife!

Think about how much your mood can change and how that affects your whole mental state and influences you physiologically. Try this as an exercise to test it out:

- Sit in a quiet room and close your eyes. Think of the worst thing that has ever happened to you. Take yourself through that moment in real time as if it is happening to you all over again. Notice how you feel and open your eyes and take in your demeanour, mood and emotion.

- Now close your eyes again and think of the best thing that has ever happened to you. Relive it moment by moment, remember how you celebrated, and soak up that feeling of elation and joy. Now open your eyes and take in your demeanour, mood and emotion.

- Notice the difference? Notice how much more positive you feel and how much you'd like to experience that again?

All you did there was to make yourself go into two different mental states, but look how powerfully those emotions affected your mentality and body. That was the power of the mind and it just demonstrated to you what it can do or, more to the point, what *you* can do.

So getting to grips with your mental state and constantly moving it into a positive place is important. It takes effort, as does anything that is worth having. Think of all the sports people out there who have to deal with their state of mind.

When you watch a sporting event and see the winners, remember that most have lost many times to attain the winning platform. It's the same in sales. You will lose many deals on your path to success, but making the success bigger than the losses is what it's all about.

I have read a lot about coaches and their comments on sports people they train. Many say that the fitness and physical condition represents 20 per cent of where they need to be: 80 per cent is mental, and if their mind is not right, they won't win.

How many times have you see a football, rugby, cricket, netball or hockey team seem to be dominant, only to completely lose it when their confidence goes? Think of tennis players and golfers who win and lose due to their mental toughness.

It's the same in sales and business. If you want to win then you have to have consistent self-belief: you need to believe in the product or service you're selling and you must have a desire to win and beat the competition.

Also remember it's about doing all the little things right as well as the big things – marginal gains. Dave Brailsford (the coach of the British cycling team that did so well at the 2012 Olympics) and Clive Woodward (the coach of the 2003 England Rugby World Cup winners) both focused on doing all the small things right in every part of fitness, diet, technique, speed, attitude and mental approach. All those small things add up to performing the whole role properly, to a world-class standard. That's what I have done with the Critical Hour for sales.

By realising that you can harness things that don't go well and turn them into things that do, setting goals and thinking positively, and knowing that change is constant, you will transform your life and ability to smash sales targets – whether you're a CEO, Sales director, sales manager or sales person.

> **High performance tips**
> - Your conscious mind is the logical/leadership part of the brain: it sees words and makes all the decisions.
> - Your subconscious mind is the creative part of the brain: it sees pictures and obeys all the decisions your conscious mind has made without question.
> - Remember that 80 per cent of what you do and achieve is down to your subconscious mind.
> - Think positive thoughts and get your conscious mind to direct you positively at all times towards your goals.

Visualisation

My account above about writing down a description of my perfect woman is effectively a form of visualisation. I visualised in detail who I wanted to meet and wrote it down, defining what my goal was.

Another form of visualisation technique can be used before you go into a meeting. Take a moment to close your eyes and visualise a positive outcome. For example, the prospect saying, 'I would like to proceed as soon as possible' or 'How quickly can we start?'

Visualise your Critical Hour going superbly and the prospect being totally engaged throughout. Whatever you visualise, say it in the present tense not the past – it's happening now. This is important as it is sending a command to your subconscious mind, which will then act and move towards the positive event.

To make this even more powerful, say it out loud or, if you are going into a meeting with a colleague, then go through this together, speaking positively about the outcome of the meeting in the present tense.

You see a lot of sports people go through visualisation prior to performing their action, for example, prior to a free kick in football, a golf shot, a high jump, etc. They are visualising the ball going into the back of the net in a precise place, a golf ball landing next to the pin or a really high jump and the bar staying on the stand.

High performance tips

- Before every Critical Hour shut your eyes and visualise a positive outcome to your meeting.
- Always visualise in the present tense – it's happening now!

Conclusion

I hope you have enjoyed this book and found it useful. I can assure you that if you put all of this together in your Critical Hours then you will really excel in new business sales. Remember that it is important to do it *all* – don't short-cut the process as that will lessen your chance of success.

Much of what I have described for new business sales also overlaps other sales roles but each part will also have its own set of special skills. Other roles include:

- Cold-calling to make appointments
- Outbound telesales
- Inbound telesales
- Customer service on the phone
- Desk-based account management
- Account management
- Strategic account management
- High-value complex sales
- Super complex sales (£50m+ deals that take two to three years to complete)
- Partner or alliance sales
- Channel sales
- Technical pre-sales

Then there are the skills required to be a great sales manager:

- Telesales frontline manager
- Call centre manager

- Frontline field sales manager
- Manager of a manager
- Sales leader (sales director/commercial director/ managing director, vice president, senior vice president, chief sales officer)

So I have many more books to write and I hope you'll stay with me on that journey!

Everyone has to sell

People always think of sales as the process of selling to people outside your organisation, but nowadays there is a huge amount of selling required within companies. For example, selling to a committee or board for internal budget, selling ideas or yourself to your boss, convincing other departments to participate in an initiative, trying to get your company to adopt a new methodology, convincing key people that someone you know should get a promotion – the list goes on.

All these require almost the same amount of time and process as described in the Critical Hour. The problem many people have with internal sales is that they do not have this type of process and so their ideas or requests are rejected.

In the end everyone sells, or has to sell at some time in their life, and anyone who says they don't just doesn't realise the fact.

For example, if you have a partner, then you have sold yourself at least once and someone bought you!

Good luck in your sales career!

Finally, a message to all those buyers out there!

On behalf of all the sales people in the world who get so frustrated with buyers' unreasonable behaviour, here is a list of requests that we would ask you to consider:

● If you don't like what is being presented to you and have no desire to do business with the sales person selling to you – tell them! Don't waste their time and yours if the sales person thinks you're interested.

● Don't ask for a proposal if you're not interested. You will be opening yourself up to call after call and email after email, as the sales person tries to get hold of you.

● If you say you're interested in a Critical Hour meeting then don't ignore all communication from the sales person after the meeting. Respond to them.

● If you receive a proposal, please acknowledge it and let the sales person know when you'll get back to them.

● Just communicate with a sales person and let them know what's going on. Once you have expressed an interest you will be logged in their pipeline, and become the subject of conversation in sales meetings, and expectations will be raised. It is much less hassle for you and less demanding of your time if you simply inform a sales person of what is happening at your end.

● If nothing is happening at your end to progress a deal, then let the sales person know.

● Managing a sales person's expectations will lead to a smooth and hassle-free sales process and a good relationship throughout a deal.

● Let sales people know your budget so they can cut their

cloth accordingly or walk away if there is nothing they can do. There is no point letting a sales person do a lot of work, only for you to not have the budget.

● If you like what the sales person is offering but need to get internal buy-in, then do this in partnership with the sales person rather than just asking for a brochure and then distributing accordingly to relevant colleagues.

Index